Worth It

Chris Morphew

thegoodbook
COMPANY

For Caely

Worth It: Following Jesus When Life Feels Complicated

© Chris Morphew, 2025

Published by:
The Good Book Company

thegoodbook.com | thegoodbook.co.uk
thegoodbook.com.au | thegoodbook.co.nz | thegoodbook.co.in

Cover design by Drew McCall

ISBN: 9781802541274 | JOB-007972 | Printed in India

Contents

CHAPTER 1

Life to the Full

"I have come that they may have life,
and have it to the full."
—Jesus of Nazareth

"It just feels overwhelming, you know?"

He sat slumped at the bottom of the little plastic slide usually reserved for our church's preschoolers, eyes down on his feet. All around him, the rest of the youth group stood chatting and eating ice cream and dropping in and out of the impromptu volleyball game someone had started—but Ethan had other things on his mind. For the last 20 minutes, he'd been giving me the latest in a series of updates on his life and school and parents and everything else that was weighing on him.[1]

He'd been coming along to youth group for a few years now and, somewhere along the way, he'd decided

---

1 Full disclosure: I've changed some of the details here to keep this particular young person anonymous—but the truth is, it's just one of so many similar stories I could tell you.

that Jesus really was who he said he was. And while becoming a follower of Jesus had made an incredible, positive difference in Ethan's life, it had also created a whole bunch of new complications and challenges.

His parents weren't exactly *against* his faith, but they didn't really get it either. ("My dad calls youth group 'the cult'—which is a joke, obviously, but it still shows you what he thinks about it.")

School was worse. Ethan's mostly atheist friends swung back and forth between honest confusion and outright derision. ("They actually *do* think I've joined a cult.") And when it came to his LGBTQIA+ friends, things were even more complicated. They didn't just feel confused; they felt *betrayed*. How could Ethan join a religion full of bigots and homophobes?

Despite all that, Ethan remained fiercely committed to his friends. But there were times when that commitment felt like way too much to carry on his own—not so much because of what they thought of his faith but because of all the *other* stuff his friends were going through.

Over the past several months, I'd started to get a sense of the main characters in Ethan's school life. One friend's parents were going through a messy divorce. Another friend was struggling with depression and anxiety. Another had what sounded uncomfortably like an eating disorder but was refusing to talk to anyone about it. Another friend, biologically female, had recently started going by he/they pronouns and was currently at war with their parents, who'd been hesitant to embrace the change.

"And I just—" Ethan started, and then broke off, rubbing his eyes. "I'm doing the best I can, but I still don't... I just feel like I never know what to say. Like, I'm not a counsellor, you know? They have all these questions and I just don't really know how to answer them."

Meanwhile, he still had plenty of questions of his own. Questions about life and faith and God and how all those pieces were meant to fit together.

In his search for answers, he'd started reading the Bible for himself—but, to him at least, that only seemed to make things worse. He'd started running into all kinds of confusing references to violence and slavery and the mistreatment of women. In some places, God seemed as generous and kind and loving and welcoming as he'd always thought—but a few pages later, it often seemed like a different story.

So what was my friend meant to do with all that?

The whole reason we were sitting here, having this conversation, was that somewhere along the way he'd caught a glimpse of the life that Jesus held out to him, and it had seemed like the most beautiful, most compelling news in the whole world. But had that all just been a blip? A momentary delusion? In the middle of all the complexity and challenge of real life, could he actually trust that "the good news about Jesus"[2] really was as good as it had first seemed?

The same question goes for us. Can we?

Living in strange days

It's a pretty rough time to be a young person.

Actually, I guess it's just a pretty rough time to be a person in general.

And, look, I know people will say that's always been true—that every generation has had its challenges, that being human has pretty much *always* been hard—but still, any way you look at it, we're living in incredibly challenging, complex times.

For one thing, we've never had more options for wiping ourselves off the face of the earth, whether it's through nuclear war, climate catastrophe, cyberterrorism, the rise of artificial intelligence, or the next global pandemic. As one scientist put it, "The planet will survive; the question is, will we?"[3]

And while technology has brought humanity closer together than ever before, opening up the possibility for us to all work together to face these challenges, let's be honest—that's not exactly what we see most of the time.

Older generations—Millennials and Gen X—grew up with the idea that *progress* was just a thing our species

---

2 Mark 1:1

3 Katharine Hayhoe, *Saving Us: A Climate Scientist's Case for Hope and Healing in a Divided World* (Atria/One Signal Publishers, 2021), p. 65.

was inevitably going to keep on achieving. They were raised on these shining ideals of a future where science, technology and education were going to solve all the world's problems and usher in a wondrous new era of peace, justice and harmony. Not that there wouldn't be challenges along the way, but most people just kind of assumed things were inevitably going to keep getting better.

But if you're a young person today, my guess is that this is not how you see things—because *you've* arrived on the planet just in time to see so many of those bright, sparkly promises crashing and burning in front of you.

You've seen how the same technology that's connected us all more closely together is also being used to push us further apart.

You've seen politics get more and more polarised, to the point where it feels like all anyone knows how to do anymore is yell at each other.

You've seen people at war with each other online—and in the streets—over issues of race, religion, gender, sexuality, climate, the treatment of refugees, and on and on. And you've seen *literal* wars break out across the world, with the very real potential to spill over into even broader, more devastating conflicts.

In almost every area of life, from politics to professional sport to Hollywood to the church, you've seen trusted institutions and beloved public figures exposed as violent, abusive and corrupt.

And, turning up the dials on all of this stuff, you've grown up in a world where the internet—and with it, most of the news and opinions we're exposed to—has become dominated by more and more sophisticated algorithms, designed not to expand our horizons, or expose us to new perspectives, or even point us to the truth but to keep us glued to our screens by any means necessary.

Which, it turns out, often means keeping us angry. As journalist Johann Hari explains, "On average, we will stare at something negative and outrageous for a lot longer than we will stare at something positive and calm … So an algorithm that prioritises keeping you glued to the screen will—unintentionally but inevitably—prioritise outraging and angering you. If it's more enraging, it's more engaging."[4]

Throw in the rise of artificial intelligence, and it's getting harder and harder to know not just *what's* real but even *who's* real online. Is it any wonder that it feels impossible to have meaningful conversations about the things we disagree on?

And in the mix of all that, you've seen—and likely felt—the impact of some truly disturbing mental health trends in recent years. Psychology professor Jean M. Twenge puts it starkly: "Every indicator of mental health and psychological well-being has become more negative among teens and young adults since 2012."[5]

---

4   Johann Hari, *Stolen Focus: Why You Can't Pay Attention* (Bloomsbury Publishing, 2023), p. 125-126.

5   Jean M. Twenge, *Generations: The Real Differences Between Gen Z,*

Meanwhile, the World Health Organisation has recently identified loneliness as a "global public health concern" with the potential to spiral into a worldwide epidemic.[6] In one recent study, more than 1 million teenagers in 37 countries were asked if they agreed with statements like "I feel lonely at school" and "I feel awkward and out of place at my school"—and in 36 out of 37 countries, the results showed an increase in school loneliness over the past decade.[7]

I could keep going, but I think you get it.

Is Jesus worth it?

Meanwhile, if you're someone who's trying to follow Jesus in the middle of all this—or if you're at least seriously considering it—that carries a whole other set of challenges.

Plenty of people see Christianity as outdated at best and bigoted or dangerous at worst—not just unhelpful in the face of all this complexity but actively contributing to the problem. Being a follower of Jesus can make you feel out of step with your friends and family, and with society in general.

All of which might leave you wondering, *Is following Jesus really worth it?*

Millennials, Gen X, Boomers, and Silents—and What They Mean for America's Future (Atria Books, 2023), p. 392.

6   Sarah Do Couto, "Global News: Loneliness is now a 'global public health concern,' says WHO", https://globalnews.ca/news/10095898/loneliness-global-public-health-concern-who/ (accessed 12 Dec. 2023).

7   Twenge, *Generations*, p. 405-406.

Is the good news about Jesus good enough to be worth all the hassle that comes with it?

Is Jesus' teaching still relevant 2,000 years on?

Jesus said he had come to bring abundant life: "I have come that they may have life, and have it to the full."[8] Is that a promise you can actually count on him to follow through on?

Can following Jesus *really* make a positive difference in your life?

I've spent years wrestling through these same questions myself—and what I've come to believe is that, in the end, all those questions are really just different ways of asking the same question:

Can I trust him?

And so that's the question I want to spend the rest of this book exploring.

First, I want to show you why I'm convinced that, no matter how good you already think the good news of Jesus is, it's *better*—that the story the Bible tells about God and humanity really is the most breathtakingly beautiful, life-giving, and *true* way to understand the universe and your place in it.

Then we'll explore what it looks like to fully lean into this story—to move beyond knowing *about* Jesus towards actually *knowing* Jesus for yourself. We'll consider what it means to experience his love and care

---

8 John 10:10

and faithfulness not just as ideas but as the heartbeat of your everyday life.

Finally, we'll pull all that together and start figuring out how you can let your relationship with Jesus transform your relationships with everyone else—and how, as you stick with him, he'll help you navigate the challenges of our uncertain world in a way that nothing and no one else can.

But before we get into any of that, we need to go right back to the beginning and talk about the only thing that's going to make any of the rest of this make sense.

We need to talk about the most important discovery that any of us can ever make.

CHAPTER 2

The Most Important Discovery

*"The most important discovery you will ever make is
the love the Father has for you."*
—Pete Greig

Here's what you need to know, above and beyond and before anything else:

You are loved.

You are loved with a love so huge and wild and expansive, it defies description or explanation. My words are going to fall so far short here, but since this love is the foundation of *everything else*, I feel like I at least need to give it a shot.

This love is the truest thing about you.[1] It's what defines who you are at the deepest, most profound level—because whatever doubts you might have about your place in the world, and whatever anybody else says, the Creator of the universe, the God of everything, the one who has the ultimate power and authority to say how much you matter, says you matter *infinitely*.

And that infinite, immeasurable value and dignity and worth is not something you need to earn or deserve or strive for or prove or measure up to. No success or failure or trophy or grade or other person's opinion can shift it a single inch—because it's all a gift. It's yours already. It's hardwired into your body, fixed deep in your bones, encoded in your DNA. This extraordinary value and significance is just *who you are*—because the one true King of heaven and earth has created you on purpose, imprinted you with his very own image, and crowned you with glory and honour.[2]

And to be clear, I'm not just talking about people in general here.

I'm talking about *you*.

Before the beginning of the universe, God had you in mind. The vast, beautiful story he's weaving together through all of time and space and history would be incomplete without you in it. You are an unceasing spiritual being with an eternal destiny in God's great

---

1 David Lomas, *The Truest Thing About You: Identity, Desire, and Why It All Matters* (David C. Cook, 2014), p. 108.
2 Genesis 1:26-27; Psalm 8:5

universe.[3] The same God who has numbered every star in the sky has also made you by hand and numbered every hair on your head.[4]

You are here on purpose—and you are here *for* a purpose. You have been created to partner with God in ruling and caring for the universe he's made, and blessing the people in it—to spend eternity filling up on the deep riches of God's love, and reflecting that love out into the world around you.[5]

And what's so important to understand is that the love I'm describing here is not just a thing God *does*; it's who God *is*.[6]

The deepest truth in the universe

The idea of the Trinity—that there's *one* God, but that he exists in three Persons: Father, Son and Holy Spirit—is one of the most mind-bending ideas in the whole Christian faith. But it's well worth the headache, because here's what it means:

Love isn't just something God *started* doing one day and might stop doing sometime in the future. It's the fundamental truth about God's identity. It's what's been going on within God's own three-in-one self—between Father, Son and Spirit—for all eternity.

---

3 This description comes from the writer Dallas Willard, quoted by John Ortberg in *Soul Keeping: Caring for the Most Important Part of You* (Zondervan, 2014), p. 19.

4 Psalm 139:13-14; Luke 12:7

5 Genesis 1:28; Matthew 22:36-40

6 1 John 4:16

And so when I tell you that love is more foundational to our universe than physics or chemistry or gravity or the speed of light, that might sound like just a cute little poetic flourish I'm pulling out, but it's not. It's the actual, literal truth. God could have set stuff like chemistry up in a thousand different ways, but love is a non-negotiable, because it's just *who God is*.

This love is how God defines himself—"the compassionate and gracious God, slow to anger, abounding in love and faithfulness, maintaining love to thousands, and forgiving wickedness, rebellion and sin".[7] And over and over again, all through history, this is who God has proven himself to be in his relationship with his people, and in his faithfulness to his promises.

Everything God has ever said or ever will say, everything he's ever done or ever will do, every instruction he's ever given or command he's handed down, it *all* flows from the exact same place: God's endless, perfect, others-focused, self-giving love.[8]

This love shields and protects, it drives out fear, it never fails.[9]

It's like the love of a devoted mother, cradling her newborn baby.[10]

It's like the love of a compassionate father, sprinting out to meet his runaway kid, letting all their failures fall

---

7 Exodus 34:7

8 Which I imagine raises a few questions. Hang in there. We'll get to them.

9 Psalm 5:12; 1 John 4:18; Psalm 36:5-7

10 Isaiah 49:15

to the dust because he's just so desperately glad to have them home again.[11]

This love is personal. It's a love that can be *known*, a love that can be *relied on*. But it's also a love that *surpasses knowledge*—a love so far beyond any other love that exists that you can't just *think* your way there. You need to *experience* it.[12]

As one writer put it, "The most important discovery you will ever make is the Father's love, and it's just that—a discovery. It cannot be taught. It has to be discovered, and everything else flows from that discovery."[13]

Too good to be true?

And, listen, if you're thinking this all seems kind of unbelievable—more like wish-fulfilment than actual reality—I absolutely get it. In a world like ours—a world so full of heartbreak and disappointment and betrayal and broken promises—it makes sense that a claim like this might leave you feeling suspicious or cynical. In the whole history of the universe, nothing even remotely as good as this has ever been true before.

And to be completely honest with you, I think I'd find the whole thing pretty vague and theoretical if it wasn't for Jesus—because it's only in him that we see all of

---

11 Luke 15:11-32

12 1 John 4:16; Ephesians 3:16-19

13 Tyler Staton, *Praying Like Monks, Living Like Fools: An Invitation to the Wonder and Mystery of Prayer* (Zondervan, 2022), p. 24. Staton is expanding on a quote from Pete Greig in *Dirty Glory: Go Where Your Best Prayers Take You* (Hodder and Stoughton, 2016), p. 53.

these extraordinary claims about the love of God, lived out in the flesh and blood of an actual human life.

In a world of corrupt leaders and institutions, here's a man who acts with complete honesty and integrity.

In a world of hypocrisy, here's a man whose actions flawlessly match his words.

In a world of oppression, here's a man who uses his power to serve.

In a world of sexism, here's a man who is radically dedicated to the rights, dignity and inclusion of women.

In a world of distraction and selfishness, here's a man who always makes time to love the person in front of him.

In a world obsessed with drawing lines to determine who's in and who's out, here's a man who constantly points to the people everyone else despises and looks down on—the ones everyone else assumes must be outside the circle of God's love and care—and says, *Them too. They're invited. They're welcomed home.*[14]

Throughout his time on earth, Jesus was constantly calling people into bigger, higher, wider, deeper, more expansive love. *Oh, so you love the people who love you? You can do better than that. Go bigger! Aim higher! Love your worst enemy. Pray for the people who make your lives miserable. Why? Because that's what God's love is like!*[15]

---

14 Mark 2:13-17; Luke 15
15 Matthew 5:43-48

The more deeply and truly we love—the more, in other words, we become like Jesus—the more we become like *God himself.*

Which is so important to realise, because there's this pervasive, toxic idea out there that the abundant love of Jesus is somehow a *different thing* to the attitude that God the Father (or, as some people want to call him, "Old Testament God") has towards us. People imagine a situation where God the Father is spiteful and cruel and out for blood—but then, thankfully, Jesus steps in and says, *Yeah, sorry about my dad, you guys. I know he's a bit much. Don't worry, I'll deal with him for you.*

As if God and Jesus are on opposite sides of a conflict.

As if Jesus had to twist his Father's arm to get him to be kind to us.

As if what God *wanted* to do was torture and destroy us, but Jesus took away his right to do that by dying on the cross in our place.

But Jesus won't let us get away with that kind of thinking. He insists that "anyone who has seen me has seen the Father" because "I and the Father are one."[16] Jesus is "the radiance of God's glory and the exact representation of his being".[17]

There is no division, no conflict, no part of God that does not have his arms stretched out toward you in love as you turn to him.

---

16   John 14:9; 10:30
17   Hebrews 1:3

When you see Jesus healing the sick, feeding the hungry, welcoming the outcast, defending the vulnerable, and welcoming lost rebels back into the family, you're seeing what *God* is like.

When you see Jesus stretched out on the cross, crying out to his Father to forgive the people pounding in the nails—when you see him laying down his life to pay the penalty for all the ways we've failed to love God and each other—you're getting a glimpse right into the heart of *God himself*:

> *This is love: not that we loved God, but that he loved us and sent his Son as an atoning sacrifice for our sins.*[18]

Which means that, no matter who you are, no matter what you've done, no matter how badly you've messed your life up, no matter who's made you feel like you're somehow beyond the reach of God's love and care and welcome, you don't need to worry about *any* of it.

You can come to God in all of your brokenness and messiness and failure and insecurity and know *exactly* how he will treat you—because, in Jesus, he has already shown you the incredible lengths he was willing to go to, to welcome you home to himself.

A truth you can't outgrow

Maybe the most famous Bible expert of the 20th century was a man named Karl Barth.

Barth's published writing stretched to over six million words. As a theology professor in Germany in the

---

18 1 John 4:10

1930s, he pushed back against Hitler's attempts to lure German Christians into pledging allegiance to the Nazi Party. Later in life, he even made the front cover of *Time* magazine.

It's said that towards the end of his career, Barth was asked if there was any way he could sum up everything he'd learned about God over the course of his life; what was the most profound, most important, most valuable insight he could offer?

He thought about it for a moment, then answered in the words of a song his mother had taught him as a child:

"Jesus loves me, this I know; for the Bible tells me so."

This was the same song my dad used to sing over me while he rocked me to sleep as a newborn baby—and to be honest, if that was all I'd ever learned about Jesus, it would have been enough.

Because at the end of all my searching, at the end of all my questions about the pain and complexity of life (even the unanswered ones), I just keep coming back to this same simple truth—that Jesus shows us a God we can trust.

Any meaningful relationship with God needs to start here: with the deep assurance that he's good and kind and faithful—and that he loves you.

CHAPTER 3

The Good News about God's Judgment

*"He will come again to judge the living
and the dead."*
—The Apostles' Creed

I wonder if, as you read the last chapter, you noticed an objection rising in your mind, or an uneasy feeling bubbling up in your stomach.

Because, sure, the Bible has a lot to say about God's love—but that's not the *whole* story, is it? What about everything the Bible says about hell and sin and judgment and all that stuff?

Doesn't that prove that God isn't *all* loving?

And doesn't that make God's love for us a whole lot harder to trust?

If that's what God is like, maybe he's not worth following after all.

"I don't believe in a God of judgment"

Some people try to get around this problem by just denying it. They'll say, "I don't believe in a God of judgment; I believe in a God of love".

Which might feel really kind and friendly and inclusive, but it doesn't actually get us very far—because the thing about real people is that you don't get to change their identities just by imagining them differently. They are who they are. Which means that, just like with any other real person, God's identity isn't something we get to *decide*; it's something we need to *discover*.

So how do we discover who God really is?

Well, let's go back to the idea of a "God of love"—how do we know *that* to be true?

Obviously, many people across many faith traditions would agree with the idea that God is *loving*—that he's merciful and kind to us. But as the writer Timothy Keller points out, the idea that God *is* love—that God's love is the core definition of God's character, the thing that *everything else* flows from—originates uniquely with the Bible.[1]

And that same Bible also has plenty to say about God's judgment:

1 Timothy Keller, *The Reason for God: Belief in an Age of Scepticism*, p. 81-83.

The LORD is our judge.[2]

It is God who judges: he brings one down, he exalts another.[3]

The LORD takes his place in court; he rises to judge the people.[4]

He will judge between many peoples.[5]

"He summons the heavens above, and the earth, that he may judge his people.[6]

[God] is ready to judge the living and the dead.[7]

People are destined to die once, and after that to face judgment.[8]

There's just no getting around it.

When Jesus famously said, "Do not judge, or you too will be judged",[9] his point was not to say that judgment is *bad*, just that it's *not our job*—it's God's.

All through the Bible, we discover that God is love—and all through the Bible, we discover that God is not just *a* judge, but *the* judge of the whole world.

Which, understandably, you might not like the sound of. But what I want to spend the rest of this chapter

---

2 Isaiah 33:22
3 Psalm 75:7
4 Isaiah 3:13
5 Micah 4:3
6 Psalm 50:4
7 1 Peter 4:5
8 Hebrews 9:27
9 Matthew 7:1

showing you is that this is actually *incredibly good news*—that, far from being the *opposite* of God's love, God's judgment is one of the most profound and beautiful ways that God *demonstrates* his love for us—that, as upside down as it might sound, God's judgment is actually one of the greatest reasons in the world to trust him.

In the beginning...

On the opening pages of the Bible, we find a true story about the first human beings that's really a true story about all of us.

In the story, God creates a man and a woman, and he puts them in a garden with two trees in front of them: the "tree of life" and "the tree of the knowledge of good and evil". They're invited to eat freely from the first tree—but warned to stay away from the second one.[10]

These two trees present the first people with a choice about how they're going to respond to God's love and care and provision for them. It's the same choice we *all* wake up to, one way or another, every single day of our lives.

Eating from the tree of life represents God's invitation to keep on trusting in his love for them enough to live the way he calls them to live—to keep on reaching out and taking the abundant, unending life that God freely offers them.

---

10 Genesis 3:7-22

Eating from the tree of the knowledge of good and evil represents the choice to *stop* trusting in God's love for them—to turn their backs on the life God offers them, and to seize control of life for themselves.

But why would they ever make *that* choice? Why would they break themselves apart from the God who made them and loves them?

For the exact same reason the rest of us do.

Unwillingness to trust

I've heard that the 16th-century priest Ignatius of Loyola described sin as an *unwillingness to trust that what God wants for me is only my deepest happiness—* which might seem like a strange way to talk about it, but actually, I think it makes all the sense in the world.

Think about it:

If we were *fully* convinced that God loved us, and that he was for us—

If we *fully* believed, deep down in our bones, that God was relentlessly good and kind and committed to us—not necessarily to our shallow, surface-level gratification, but to our *deepest* joy and flourishing—

If we *really* trusted that "the way God tells us to live" and "the right thing to do" and "what's best for us" and "the way to find true freedom and happiness" aren't four different categories, but that they're only ever always the *exact same thing*—

If we truly and completely believed all that, then *of course* we'd do whatever God asked us to do. It would be the most natural thing in the world. Giving up on obeying a God like that would be as absurd to us as giving up on breathing.

The trouble is, that's not our experience. We *don't* fully trust in God's love for us. We believe it, but we don't believe it. And so, rather than letting go and letting God drive, we cling to the steering wheels of our lives with white knuckles.[11]

We see this in the story of the first people. When God's enemy slithers into the garden, he doesn't come after God's children with violence or threats—or even with an outright instruction to do something wrong. His plan of attack is a subtle line of questions and deceptions designed to undermine their trust.[12]

Did God really say you couldn't have that? If he's really a loving Father, why is he holding out on you? He's not who he says he is. He's holding you back from being your authentic self. The only way you'll ever be fulfilled and free is by taking control for yourself.

The man and woman consider his words.

They believe the lie. They eat from that second tree.

But, like I said, this isn't just a story about those people back then.

---

11 David Benner, *Surrender to Love: Discovering the Heart of Christian Spirituality* (IVP, 2015), p. 66-67.

12 Genesis 3:1-5

Over and over again, we make the same choice the first people made: we believe the lie that God doesn't really love us, that we can't really trust him, that he's somehow holding out on us. And so we turn our backs on God's love and care and guidance, and do things our way instead.

Instead of freely and open-handedly loving God and the people around us, safe in the knowledge that God will keep filling us up with *his* love, we turn our focus inward. We become preoccupied with our own self-protection and self-fulfilment—which leads us to do all kinds of damage to ourselves and to the people around us.

We bend the truth to protect our reputation. We exclude the person who feels like too much effort. We choose greed over generosity, bitterness over forgiveness, holding on to our own comfort instead of reaching out in love.

And so our fractured relationships with God spill over into fractured relationships with each other and the fracturing of the whole world.

It's not so much that everything's wrong; it's that there's something wrong with everything.[13] The beauty and the brokenness are all blended together—and in our modern world, we've got a front-row seat to all of it.

---

13 I owe this observation to pastor and author Jeff Manion.

Drinking from the firehose

It's 6:00 a.m.

I wake up, grab my phone to silence the alarm, and start scrolling without really meaning to.

Swipe.

My friend beams back at me, flashing an engagement ring.

Swipe.

A weeping father cradles the lifeless body of his child in the bombed-out shell of their home.

Swipe.

My twin nephews laugh and shriek as my dad pushes them around in a wheelbarrow.

Swipe.

Another school shooting.

Swipe.

$1 vs $1000 garlic bread. The $1000 version looks incredible—but honestly, the $1 version still looks pretty good.

Swipe.

A clip from a podcast. Two guys with beards, agreeing with each other that climate change is a hoax.

I put my phone down and roll out of bed, the image of that dad crying over his dead kid rising to the top of the swirl of images. I feel vaguely uneasy, my body prodding me instinctively to do something to help, but he's halfway across the world in the middle of a warzone and I don't even know his name.

Our only hope

What are we supposed to *do* with all this? With this firehose of beauty and brokenness that comes blasting at us every single day?

The Bible gives us a compelling origin story for the mess we've all been born into—but what are we meant to do about it, now that we're here?

Where can we turn to make sense of all the pain and suffering and injustice and heartache in the world? What hope do we have in a world this complex and broken—a world where trying to hold on to peace and justice is like trying to catch smoke?

According to Jesus, our only hope is in God's judgment.

Which might sound like the complete opposite of help—until you realise what this judgment actually looks like.

See, part of our problem is that when we hear *judgment*, we think *judgmental*.

We think prejudice, hypocrisy, a failure of empathy, someone jumping to unfair conclusions about us without taking the time to see things from our point of view.

And so if we take all that baggage and load it into our

view of *God's* judgment, of course it's going to seem like bad news.

But that's not what God's judgment looks like.

When the Bible talks about God's judgment, it's talking about his *justice*. In fact, in the Old Testament's original Hebrew language, those two words—justice and judgment—are one and the same: *mishpat*.

God's *mishpat* is the complete *opposite* of the prejudice and hypocrisy we so often associate with "judgment". It's not about God sitting up on a cloud somewhere with a clipboard and a frown, waiting for an excuse to blast you.

It's about drawing a line between right and wrong so that justice can be done.

It's about caring for the poor and the vulnerable.

It's about making sure everybody has what they need to thrive.

It's about speaking up for people who can't speak up for themselves.

It's about the God of perfect love looking out at all the world's darkness and despair, at all of humanity's evil and violence and self-destruction, at all the things in this world that run you down and wear you out and break your heart, and saying, *This has got to stop.*

God's judgment, his justice, is about God coming to *save the world*—to take all the wrong things in our world and make them right again.

Which brings us to hell—which, like God's judgment, is probably not quite what you think it is.

The truth about hell

When you open the Bible and see Jesus talking about hell, I'm guessing the image that first drops into your mind is some kind of underground torture chamber scenario. Caves. Lava. Maybe some demons with pitchforks.

But Jesus' original audience would have pictured something quite different—because that English word hell is a translation of the original Greek word, *Gehenna*—which, in turn, comes from the Hebrew place name, *Ge Hinnom*, or "Valley of Hinnom".

And Gehenna, the Valley of Hinnom, was not an underground torture chamber. It was an actual valley, just outside the city of Jerusalem in Israel.

Jerusalem was a walled city on a hill, built to be a place of safety, security and community. It was the king's city and, most importantly, it was home to the temple, where people could go to be with God.

Down below, outside the city wall, was the Valley of Hinnom, a place that was all tied up with one of the darkest times in the history of God's people.

Centuries earlier, in the Valley of Hinnom, the people of Jerusalem had burned their children alive as sacrifices to Baal and Molek, the false gods of the nations around them. Eventually, their evil ways caught up with them: Jerusalem was invaded and destroyed, and the bodies of God's people were thrown down into the same valley where they'd sacrificed their children.[14]

Obviously, this is all incredibly grim. And you can see why, to Jesus' original audience, the Valley of Hinnom was a pretty effective way of describing *the place you don't want to end up.*

But many scholars believe that the metaphor doesn't end there—because there's evidence to suggest that, eventually, this same valley had become a dumping ground for Jerusalem's garbage and sewage.

Now, clearly, a garbage dump is a terrible place to *be*. But when you think about it, it's still a great place to *have*—because it means you don't have to let your garbage just keep piling up in your homes and your streets. You can take all that gross junk that doesn't belong and get it out of the city.

Which is exactly what Jesus has promised to come back and do—not just for a city but for *the whole universe.*

Jesus has promised that one day he'll return to earth to bring ultimate, once-and-for-all justice; to take all the gross junk that doesn't belong in God's good world—all of the death and destruction and evil and violence that we've created—and get rid of *all of it*; to gather it all up and cast it out into the cosmic garbage dump.

Because God is perfect and holy—because he is so profoundly loving and good—he will not let evil continue in our world forever. There will come a day

---

14   Jeremiah 7:30-34; 2 Kings 25

when it will all be over—when death and mourning and crying and pain will be nothing but old stories we tell each other about the way things *used* to be.[15]

This is *good news*, right?

And it gets better.

Barrelling towards Gehenna

Like I said, the other crucial upshot of Jesus' Gehenna/ Valley of Hinnom metaphor is, *This is not a place you want to end up.* Not because you're going to be tortured by demons or whatever—but follow the metaphor:

Being *inside* the city of Jerusalem meant peace, joy, safety, community and friendship with God.

Being *outside*, in the valley, meant *separation* from all of that.

And Jesus says that left to our own devices, this is the reality we're all facing; we're all barrelling down the road that dead-ends in that valley—in the place of death and separation from God's love.

It's not that God thinks we're garbage. (More on this in the next chapter.) But if Jesus is going to bring ultimate justice—if he's going to bring a permanent end to all evil, everywhere—then he needs to get rid of all the causes of that evil, right?

And the truth is, that includes all of us. We've all made the same choice the first man and woman did. We've

---

15   Revelation 21:4

all sinned and fallen short of God's glory.[16] One way or another, we've all denied and rejected God's love for us and responded by taking life into our own hands. We're not just the victims of a world gone wrong; we're also the perpetrators—and so what verdict could a true God of justice possibly pronounce over our lives other than *guilty*?

But thanks to Jesus, that's not the end of the story. Because, yes, in his great love, Jesus is coming to get the garbage out of the world—but first, Jesus came to get the garbage out of *us*.

Getting the garbage out of us

Jesus is the one person who fully and completely trusted in his Father's love for him—and who, out of that place of absolute trust, lived the perfect life of love for God and others that we were created for but have fallen short of. He was the one person who God could rightly declare *not guilty*.

Instead, Jesus went to the cross. He was arrested by the authorities, convicted in an unjust trial, whipped and beaten, hauled outside Jerusalem like garbage, and given a criminal's execution. But what humanity meant for evil, God meant for good.[17]

Through his death, Jesus paid the debt for our guilty verdicts, cancelling every charge against us.[18] He took all the garbage of our sin onto himself, giving up his

16 Romans 3:23
17 Genesis 50:20
18 Colossians 2:13-15

life for all the ways we make a mess of ours.[19] And then, through his resurrection, he proved his authority over even death itself.

Which means that now, if we put our faith in him—if we turn back to God and receive the rescue that Jesus died to bring us—we can look forward to the day when Jesus returns to judge the world, with complete assurance that God has declared us as *not guilty* as Jesus himself. Not because of our track record but because of his.[20]

In the meantime, even that *faith* part isn't something we need to achieve on our own. When we turn back to God and believe this good news, he gives us his Holy Spirit—God himself, right here with us—to drive the truth of his love deeper and deeper into our hearts, transforming us into people who more and more naturally trust his love enough to live his way while we wait for his return.

Jesus answers our heart's cry for justice with real, tangible, certain hope for a future where *all* the world's wrongs are made right—which means we can trust him, not only with our own personal futures but with the future of the whole universe.

---

19   1 Peter 2:24; 1 Corinthians 15:3
20   Romans 3:21-26

CHAPTER 4

Better than You Think

*"Many Christians have been taught only
half the story."*
—Jon Tyson

Awhile back, I was reading through Mark's biography of Jesus with one of my fifth-grade Christian Studies classes at school, and we got to the part where Mark sums up Jesus' message to the crowds:

> *Jesus went into Galilee, proclaiming the good news of God. "The time has come," he said. "The kingdom of God has come near. Repent and believe the good news!"* [1]

"Okay," I said, looking up from my Bible, "what do we already know about this? What do you think this 'good news of God' is all about?"

Most of the class hesitated—but from the front row, one hand shot into the air. It belonged to a girl who

---

1 Mark 1:14-15

I knew had grown up in church her whole life, whose knowledge of the Bible could rival plenty of full-grown adults. I nodded at her to answer.

"You're a sinner," she told me.

Across the room, someone choked on a mouthful of water.

"No, I mean—not just him," the girl clarified. "We all are. You have this heavy burden called sin, which means you *should* end up in hell forever after you die. But thankfully Jesus died for you, so now, if you put your faith in him, then when you die, you can go to be with him in heaven instead."

She beamed back at me, confident she'd nailed it.

"Great," I said, "that's a really good start."

And it really was—but on the inside, I still felt my heart sink a little bit.

Not because this kid had done anything wrong. What she'd said was true, as far as it went. It was a clear and thoughtful summary of the way she and so many of us were first introduced to the good news of Jesus.

But this all-too-common summary of the gospel has some huge gaps in it—and it massively undersells just how *incredibly good* Jesus' "good news" really is.

For one thing, it starts in the wrong place. It opens with, *Here's a problem you didn't think you had—but don't worry, here's a solution you didn't think you needed*, which is not exactly the world's most inspiring sales pitch.

Then there's the fact that this summary of the gospel is almost entirely about what happens *after you die*—and so it's bound to leave you wondering how this information is supposed to make much difference to your life before then.

It also gives the impression that Jesus' ultimate plan is to float us all away to a final destination *somewhere else*—to some vague, half-real cloud dimension called "heaven"—which is not at all what Jesus taught.

And, maybe worst of all, this summary of the gospel almost completely ignores both the beginning and the ending of the true story God is *actually* telling.

Starting at the beginning

Yes, absolutely, the Bible is clear that we've all run out on the God who made us, that we're all in desperate need of his rescue, and that our fractured relationship with God is such a huge deal that the *only* way to put things right was for Jesus to give up his life in our place.

Those things are true, but they're not where the story begins.

The story doesn't start with sin; it starts with love—with God hand-crafting humanity in his own image to spend the rest of forever sharing in his perfect love and partnering with him to rule and govern his good creation.[2]

And this is absolutely critical.

---

2 Genesis 1:26-28; 2:7

If we skip past all this and start the story with sin, we give the impression that our fundamental identity is "you are terrible"—which is not at all what the Bible teaches.

When Jesus was confronted by a bunch of self-righteous religious people, demanding to know why he was spending so much time with "tax collectors and sinners"—with people they just assumed were too fundamentally terrible for God to want anything to do with—Jesus explained, "It is not the healthy who need a doctor, but the sick".[3]

Jesus describes sin as *sickness*.

And what I want you to notice here is that identifying someone as sick is not a statement about their fundamental identity; it's a statement about *how* they are, not *who* they are.

A person with cancer is not *fundamentally* a "cancer patient". Their cancer is not their deepest, truest self; it's a *malfunctioning* of their deepest, truest self—a corruption of normal cellular activity. It's extremely serious. It needs to be dealt with or it's going to kill them. But their cancer is not, at the deepest level, who they are. Who they are is a *person* in dire need of a doctor to restore them to the fullness of life they were created for.

And the same, Jesus says, is true of us, in all the mess of our sin:

We are desperately sick and in need of a doctor.

---

3 Mark 2:15-17

We are hopelessly lost and in need of a rescuer.[4]

We are chained up in prison and in need of liberation.[5]

We are dead and in need of resurrection.[6]

Our situation could not be more serious—but these are all statements about *how* we are, not *who* we are.

Your fundamental identity is not *sinner*.

Your fundamental identity is *made in the image of God*.

The reason the breakdown of our relationship with God is so unfathomably tragic is that it's the fracturing of something so unfathomably great.

If I draw a little stick figure on a scrap of paper and then throw that paper in the bin, I doubt anyone is going to shed any tears. But if I set fire to the Mona Lisa or put a wrecking ball through Michelangelo's David, it's a different story, because those things are priceless masterpieces.

Which, according to the Bible, is also what *you* are.[7]

And human beings aren't just God's greatest sculptures. We're God's sculptures of *himself*—reflections of his character—installed here on earth so that anyone who looks at us can say, "Oh, so *that's* what God is like".

The reason your sin and rebellion are so disastrous is because you're defacing the priceless artwork you were

---

4 Luke 19:10
5 Luke 4:16-19
6 John 5:24
7 Psalm 8:5-6; 139:13-14

truly created to be, and defaming the artist who gave you that identity and purpose in the first place.

Getting the beginning of the story right doesn't make our sin and rebellion any less serious; if anything, it shines an even brighter spotlight on the betrayal and tragedy of it all.

But what it *also* does is set us up to make better sense of the whole rest of the story:

Jesus' purpose in dying for you wasn't to make a way for God to love you even though what he *actually* thinks of you is that you're horrible and disgusting; Jesus died because God *already* loved you.[8]

And God's great plan for the future isn't just to save you from hell or get you into heaven; it's to restore *everything* that's been lost and broken as we've turned away from him, and to welcome us back into the fullness of life we were always made for.[9]

Which brings us to the *other* part of the story that so often gets left out.

The true end of the story

If you ask most followers of Jesus what they think is going to happen to them when they die, they'll tell you that they're going to go to heaven to be with Jesus.

Which, sure, is *part* of what the Bible teaches. When Jesus' friend Paul talked about death, he described it as

---

8 John 3:16
9 Colossians 1:19–20; 2 Peter 3:13; Revelation 21:5

leaving this life and going to be with Jesus,[10] and when Jesus was on the cross, he told one of the criminals dying next to him, "Truly I tell you, today you will be with me in paradise".[11]

So yes, anyone who puts their trust in Jesus can look forward to being with him in heaven after they die—but that's not our final destination.

As we've seen already, the great story of God and humanity is the story of how Jesus is on a rescue mission to renew and restore and redeem *this world*. This place—the physical universe you're living in, here and now—is where the action is, and it's where it *always will be*.

We don't need to go anywhere else to be with Jesus, because he's coming to us.[12]

Right now, Jesus is patiently waiting to give each one of us all the opportunity we need to turn back to him and let him rescue us; after all, he doesn't want anyone to perish, but everyone to come back home to him.[13]

But one day, Jesus will return. And when he does, "the dead will hear the voice of the Son of God and those who hear will live".[14]

When Jesus returns, every single dead person who has ever put their trust in him will come back to life, just

---

10 Philippians 1:23
11 Luke 23:43
12 Revelation 21:2-3
13 Ezekiel 18:23; 1 Timothy 2:4; 2 Peter 3:9
14 John 5:25

like Jesus did[15]—not as ghosts or angels or whatever, but as real flesh-and-blood humans[16] with real human bodies that can no longer get sick or die, because thanks to Jesus, the power of death no longer has any authority over us.[17] "Then the saying that is written [in the Old Testament] will come true: 'Death has been swallowed up in victory.'"[18]

Those of us who are still alive when Jesus returns will just keep on living. We'll be transformed into our new, imperishable bodies without ever having to die,[19] and we'll join with everyone else in joyfully welcoming our great King Jesus back to earth.[20]

And when he returns, Jesus will renew all things,[21] setting the world free from all the damage we've done to it,[22] wiping every tear from our eyes and bringing a permanent end to all the death and mourning and crying and pain that our sin has brought into the story.[23]

Which means that, at long last, God and his people can spend the rest of forever doing what we were always meant to do: ruling with God and sharing in his abundant love, *right here on earth*.[24]

---

15   1 Corinthians 15:22-23; 1 Thessalonians 4:16
16   Luke 24:36-43
17   Romans 6:9; 1 Corinthians 15:42-44
18   1 Corinthians 15:54
19   1 Corinthians 15:51-53
20   1 Thessalonians 4:17
21   Matthew 19:28; Revelation 21:5
22   Romans 8:21-22
23   Revelation 21:4
24   Revelation 22:5

Ruling the world with God

Here's why this changes everything.

Ruling the world with God isn't just something God's people are going to start doing on some future day when Jesus returns. It begins today. Jesus is looking for disciples—for *apprentices*.

He's looking for people who will come alongside him and learn to live the way *he* lived, so that we can join with God in the renewal of all things, starting right here, right now, today.[25]

Okay. So what does that actually look like?

Well, for my friends Chris and Ali, it looked like moving their whole family to a remote part of the country and sharing the good news of Jesus with other people, so that those people can be welcomed back home into God's family too.

But that's just one example.

My friend Andrew is a doctor who goes into work every day to wage war against sickness and suffering and death.

My friend Kerryn pours countless hours into the lives of the young people at her school.

My friends Phil and Meredith started up a board games publishing company, creating fun, beautiful, sustainable games that bring families and friends together around a table.

---

25   Jon Tyson and Heather Grizzle, *A Creative Minority: Influencing Culture Through Redemptive Participation* (Heather Grizzle Pub, 2016), p. 27.

My friend Georgie is an artist who brings a little bit more order and beauty and goodness into the world every time she picks up a pencil or a paintbrush.

The students at my school all got together last year to collect a ton and a half of rice to help feed newly-resettled refugee families.

And through *all* of these things, these people are ruling the world with God. They are partnering with him in the renewal of all things. They're taking the gifts and interests and opportunities God has given them, and they're bringing light to the darkness.

So what about you?

Well, if you're trying to figure out how all this works out in your life, maybe the best question to start with is, "What do you love to do?"

What has God put in your heart that lights you up, that makes the time slip by without you even noticing, that makes you think, *I could do this forever*? And what might it look like to use *that* to shine the light of God's love and joy and peace out into the world?

Our participation in this world matters, because *this* world is the one God promises to renew and restore. All our efforts to love our neighbours, to move towards peace and justice, to create order and beauty, to serve the poor, to welcome the lonely, or to care for the planet aren't just nice ideas we've come up with; they're ways of participating in the God-given work of ruling and caring for the world. Not to try to earn God's love—we've got that already—but to keep on becoming the people we were created to be, to keep stepping into more and more of the love and joy and peace and freedom we were created for.

And when it feels like even our best efforts are messy and imperfect, and like the problems of the world feel way too big, *that's because they are*. But don't let that worry you because, remember, it's not up to us. Jesus is the one putting the whole universe back together again.

But at the same time, however clumsily and haphazardly we might pursue the life Jesus calls us to, we can rest assured that in the end, *none* of our efforts are wasted, because Jesus assures us that, when it's all said and done, *this is where the whole universe is headed*.

CHAPTER 5

How Did We Get Here?

"Jesus Christ is easily the most dominant figure in all history."
—H.G. Wells

"It feels like I'm living in the multiverse," she said.

"Okay," I replied, "I'm going to need you to explain that."

"It's like I'm living two different lives at the same time," she explained. "I come here to youth group, and to church, and it all makes so much sense, you know? Like, I really do believe it all. But then I go out into the real world and my friends just—I mean, they still respect me. But they also think I'm crazy."

"And you sometimes wonder if they're right?" I suggested.

"Well, yeah, kind of. They're like, 'You're such a good person. How can you believe all that stuff?' And sometimes I try to argue, but mostly I just don't talk about it. I just keep quiet."

I nodded, giving her space to continue. Her brow furrowed as she searched for the right words for what she wanted to say next.

"I don't get it," she said eventually. "It's like, half the time, following Jesus means believing stuff that everyone else fully supports—but then the other half, it's like we're on a different planet. The other day, my friend was like, 'I just think you're on the wrong side of history'. And it feels like—" She sighed and shrugged her shoulders. "I don't know. Like, how can I be so sure we aren't?"

The wrong side of history?

As I've been trying to show you over the past few chapters, the Bible tells a wild, beautiful, life-changing story of where history is headed—but, as you may have noticed, that's not the same story everybody is telling.

In most people's minds, I think the real story goes something like this:

Once upon a time, pretty much everyone in the Western world (Northern America, Western Europe, Australia, etc.) was a Christian. Everyone believed in God and everyone went to church.

But the further society advanced, the less religious we became. Science showed us we didn't need God to explain how the world works—and the more educated we all became, the more we realised the need to progress past the Bible's outdated vision of morality.

These days, almost all of us have moved on from Christianity. We might still believe in God or some other kind of higher power, but organised religion is something we've rightly left behind.

There are still Christians out there (mostly old people and not-very-intelligent people) but they're just the ones who refuse to get with the times. And as the years go by, and those people either die or become better educated, churches will continue getting smaller and smaller.

Christianity is on the way out—and honestly, we're probably not going to miss it that much when it's gone.

All that to say, if following Jesus makes you feel slightly out of place sometimes, that's probably not surprising.

There are plenty of places around the world where holding to the Christian faith comes with very real danger and persecution—where people are harassed and imprisoned and even killed for following Jesus.

But if you're reading this book, I'm guessing that's not your situation.

I'm guessing that, for you, the tension of following Jesus looks less like outright persecution and more like the subtle, sinking feeling that maybe that story of the inevitable decline of Christianity is *true*—that maybe we really *are* on the wrong side of history.

It's the tension of holding on to a set of values that seem pretty reasonable when you're hanging out with other followers of Jesus, but that suddenly feel kind of weird and shaky when you step out into the wider world.

It's the tension of hearing the message of Jesus and finding it so clear and compelling and beautiful—and then struggling to know what to say to your friends who see the claims of Christianity as narrow-minded and regressive and holding humanity back.

And so what do we *do* with all this?

Well, before we figure out how to move forward, I think we need to retrace our steps and take another look back at how we got here—because it turns out that, just like the commonly retold version of the gospel we spent the last chapter untangling, this commonly retold story of the rise and fall of Christianity needs some serious revision too.

The world before Jesus

Let's start with this question: what was the world like *before* Jesus arrived on earth—before the Christian faith got started in the first place?

The idea that the universe was created by a God of love who cares for his world and his people might sound like a pretty standard understanding of God. But before the 1st century, it was unique to the Israelites—God's people—and their Old Testament Scriptures.

All the other ancient creation stories back then featured multiple gods who looked a whole lot like the people who dreamed them up: angry and volatile and constantly at war with each other. According to these stories, the gods created human beings as an afterthought at best— and if you failed them, or disappointed them, or just caught them on a bad day, they'd wipe you off the map without thinking twice about it.

And so the idea that every human life is precious and valuable might seem obvious to you, but back in the ancient world, people saw things completely differently.

If you travelled back to Ancient Greece and told Plato or Aristotle or any of the other giants of ancient philosophy that every human life was equal, they would think you'd completely lost touch with reality.

Look around you! they'd say. *There are women and men, masters and slaves, wise and foolish, strong and weak. This person is richer than that person; this person is more popular; this person has more political power. Choose your category, compare any two people, and what will you find? This person has more, and that person has less— which is the exact definition of unequal! So how can you possibly claim that every human life is equally precious and valuable? What in the world are you basing that on?*[1]

---

[1] This summary is a close paraphrase of the one Glen Scrivener provides in *The Air We Breathe: How We All Came to Believe in Freedom, Kindness, Progress, and Equality* (The Good Book Company, 2022), p. 43.

To the ancient world, equality was nonsense. Slavery was just good economics. The authority of men over women was a fundamental building block of society. Consent was not even a conversation. And Plato and Aristotle both agreed that if your newborn baby was not a decent physical specimen, you could and should abandon it to die.

Concepts like "human rights" and the fundamental equality of all human beings might *seem* self-evident to us today—but their origins are unique to the Bible, grounded in the revolutionary claim that every single human being is created in the image of God.

The timeline of history

Even our understanding of *time itself* isn't self-evident— because, again, the ancient world saw things completely differently.

These pre-Christian religious systems (and even some religious traditions that still exist today) had a *cyclical* view of history. They didn't see history as *going* anywhere. The world as a whole wasn't advancing or progressing; it just moved through repeated cycles, like the seasons.

Again, just look around you: winter turns into spring, into summer, into autumn, back into winter again. You plant and then harvest, and then plant, and then harvest. Kingdoms rise and kingdoms fall. Life and death and life and death, and on and on forever.

The Old Testament, on the other hand, saw history as *headed somewhere*. It said history wasn't just endless circles; it was a line progressing forward towards a destination—towards the renewal of all things.[2]

Which means that every time you look at events mapped out on a timeline, you're looking at a uniquely *biblical* vision of history. Again, it seems like common sense to us—but at the time, it was revolutionary.

The Jesus revolution

And so in comes Jesus. He affirms all these revolutionary ideas from the Old Testament Scriptures, and then he keeps colouring in the picture, drawing people deeper and deeper into God's true vision for humanity:

I'm glad you know murder is wrong—but don't stop there; let's get to the heart of it. Let's deal with the anger inside of you that comes from that same dark place.[3]

I'm glad you know it's wrong to sleep with someone else's wife—but you can objectify and dehumanise a woman without ever laying a hand on her, so we're going to need to deal with that too.[4]

Don't just love your neighbours; love your enemies. Isn't that how God treats you?[5]

Fast-forward to the day of Jesus' resurrection, and you find him making the audacious claim that this entire story, everything God has been doing through all of

---

2 Mark Sayers, *Reappearing Church: The Hope for Renewal in the Rise of Our Post-Christian Culture* (Moody, 2019), p. 23.

3 Matthew 5:21-22

4 Matthew 5:27-30

5 Matthew 5:43-47

human history, is reaching its culmination in *him*[6]— which would be completely outrageous if he hadn't just died and come back to life again.

After Jesus rose, the Christian faith spread like wildfire across the ancient world, as more and more people accepted Jesus' offer of rescue and welcome into life and friendship with God. And with that rescue came a revolution in their thinking: history was headed somewhere, and every single human being mattered because the God of the universe *said* they mattered.

The good news of Jesus turned the world upside down.

And while there never was a magical time in history where the whole Western world went to church and everyone was a devoted follower of Jesus—people have always been more diverse and complicated than that— even so, for hundreds of years a Christian worldview permeated the West. Even people who didn't believe in Jesus tended to believe in what he taught about morality.

Over time, Jesus' revolutionary values—equality, humility, compassion, freedom, progress, love for enemies—became widely accepted to the point of being seen as *just common sense*.

Post-Christian culture

What does all this mean for us?

Well, the first thing to say is that despite the rumours of Christianity's demise, the truth is the complete

6   Luke 24:25-27, 44-45; John 5:39-40, 46

opposite. When we zoom out from our Western bubble, we discover that, from a global perspective, more people are discovering the good news of Jesus now than at any other time in history.

For those of us in the West, though, it's a different story. We're living in what's become known as a *post-Christian* culture.

This doesn't mean that Christianity has disappeared—there are still many millions of Christians living in the West. Christianity is just no longer the dominant, mainstream worldview. You don't walk down the streets of Manhattan or Sydney or London or Berlin and assume all the people passing you by follow Jesus too. You know they're far more likely to see Christianity as an outdated set of beliefs that our society has tried in the past but has now moved on from.

The thing is, though, we haven't moved on as much as we think we have. Most people who don't believe that Christianity is true still kind of *live* as if it's true.[7] They're still holding on to a bunch of Jesus' ideas and values.

For one thing, where did we discover this idea of society *moving on* in the first place? Where did we get the idea that history is not just running in circles, but heading somewhere brighter and better?

People today might deny that they believe the Bible, but they're still *deeply* committed to the biblical idea

---

7 Mark Sayers, *Disappearing Church: From Cultural Relevance to Gospel Resilience* (Moody, 2016), p. 15-16.

of progress. They still assume that history is moving forward, and they still hope for a future where justice is done and the wrong things are made right. But instead of grounding that hope in the knowledge that Jesus has come to save us, they're grounding it in the idea that *we can save ourselves*.[8]

Which, to be honest, seems like a lot of pressure—and pretty out of touch with the reality we see around us today.

Meanwhile, having come to believe that values like equality, humility, compassion, freedom, progress and love for enemies are really just common sense, our society is trying to hang on to them, while forgetting where they came from in the first place.

But as we've seen already, these values *aren't* common sense at all.

Take human rights, for example. Here's how the atheist writer Yuval Noah Harari lays it out:

> *"Human rights, just like God and heaven, are just a story that we've invented. They are not an objective reality; they are not some biological fact about homo sapiens. Take a human being, cut him open, look inside, you will find the heart, the kidneys, neurons, hormones, DNA, but you won't find any rights. The only place you find rights are in the stories that we have invented and spread around over the last few centuries. They may be very positive stories, very*

---

8 Sayers, *Reappearing Church*, p. 24.

good stories, but they're still just fictional stories that we've invented."[9]

In other words, if you cut God out of the picture—if you think he's just a story we've invented—you're removing our whole foundation for the reality of human rights. If God is fictional, human rights are fictional too.

But we still believe in them.

We're living in a culture that's trying to have one without the other—a culture that (whether we realise it or not) is trying to hold on to all of the gifts of Christianity without acknowledging the giver of those gifts. As the writer Mark Sayers puts it, we want the kingdom without the King.[10]

Where to from here?

All of which helps to explain why my friend at youth group felt like she was in such a weird spot, trying to follow Jesus today.

Because when following Jesus means believing things our culture still approves of, or living in ways that align with the values our culture is still holding on to, people will say, "Yeah, but isn't that just common sense?" and so it can be hard to see how following Jesus makes all that much difference—even though he's the one who brought those realities to light in the first place.

---

9   Yuval Noah Harari, "What Explains the Rise of Humans", https://www.ted.com/talks/yuval_noah_harari_what_explains_the_rise_of_humans/transcript (accessed 8 Jan. 2024).

10   Sayers, *Reappearing Church*, p. 23.

And when following Jesus means believing things our culture now *disapproves* of, or living in ways that align with values our culture *isn't* still holding on to, people will accuse us of being on the wrong side of progress— even though all we're doing is following the one who first showed them that progress was even a thing.

Which is not to say that any of us ever perfectly live out the way of Jesus. Christians have failed to live according to Jesus' teaching and example in all kinds of ways throughout history—and whenever that happens, we should do everything we can to apologise and make things right.

Still, if the good news of Jesus really is true, then it's *all* true—which means the bits that make us feel out of place are just as beautiful and good and important to hold on to as the bits that make us fit right in.[11]

Okay. But even if this look back at the past helps make sense of *why* following Jesus can make you feel so out of place sometimes, that still leaves us with the question of what we're supposed to *do* about it all.

How do we keep following Jesus at a time in history when most people seem pretty happy to leave him behind?

---

11 Which I realise might not seem self-evidently true to you, but we'll get into it more in the next chapter.

CHAPTER 6

Living Like
It's True

"Don't talk about it; be about it."
—Matthew Kern

If you're going to keep trusting and following Jesus through all the ups and downs of life in our anxious, complex, post-Christian moment, there are three things I think you need to feel confident about:

First, you need to be confident that the good news of Jesus really is *good*. This is what I've spent most of this book so far trying to convince you about—and I really hope that, somewhere along the way, you've found your view of God's boundless, unfailing love for you coming into clearer focus.

Second, you need to be confident that the good news of Jesus is actually *true*—that Jesus really did live and die and rise, and that he really is coming back to put our broken universe back together again. Since you've made it six chapters into a book like this, I'm going to assume you're at least partway on board with the truth of the Jesus message—but just in case it's helpful, I've included an appendix in the back titled "Can I really believe this stuff?", which outlines a bunch of the historical evidence that Jesus really is who he says he is.

But even if you're completely confident about the goodness and truth of the Jesus message, I still don't think that's enough. Because if we stop there, it's all still theoretical. And as important as the theory is, when Jesus talked about the reason he was here, he didn't say, *I have come that they may have all the facts about God perfectly arranged inside their heads.*

He said, "I have come that they may have life, and have it to the full".[1]

Which means that if you're going to confidently trust and follow Jesus in all the complexity of life, there's one more thing you need to know: not just that the good news of Jesus is good and true but that it *actually works out in real life.*

Like I've said before, God's love for you, just like anyone else's love, isn't something you can fully know just by being *taught* about it. You need to *discover* it—to *experience* it in the reality of your everyday life.

Okay. So how do we do that?

---

1 John 10:10

Be about it

There's this scene in John's Gospel that somehow slipped past me for the first couple of decades I spent following Jesus.

Jesus is teaching in the temple courts in Jerusalem, and his audience is questioning his message: "How did this man get such learning without having been taught?"[2]

Jesus replies that he didn't make this stuff up on his own—it comes from God his Father—and then he follows up with this: "Anyone who chooses to *do the will of God* will find out whether my teaching comes from God or whether I speak on my own."[3]

Not long afterwards, Jesus makes a similar claim to his followers: "If you *hold to my teaching* ... you will know the truth, and the truth will set you free."[4]

Over in Matthew's Gospel, we find Jesus wrapping up a day of teaching by saying, "Everyone who hears these words of mine and *puts them into practice* is like a wise man who built his house on the rock".[5]

Hours before his arrest, we find Jesus washing his friends' feet. He goes on to remind them that this practical example of God's love is the way they should all be treating each other—and then he follows up with these words: "Now that you know these things, you will be blessed *if you do them*."[6]

---

2 John 7:15

3 John 7:17, emphasis mine.

4 John 8:31-32, emphasis mine.

5 Matthew 7:24, emphasis mine.

6 John 13:17, emphasis mine.

Are you sensing a pattern here?

My friend Matt has an expression he likes to pull out whenever he thinks I'm spinning my wheels—when I'm full of ideas but short on action: "Don't talk about it; be about it."

Which I think is pretty close to what Jesus is getting at here: *You want to know if my teaching checks out? You want to experience more of my love in your life? Then follow me. Don't just listen to my teaching. Live as if it's true for a while, and see what happens.*

Don't talk about it; be about it.

A gift to be received

Now, here's what I'm absolutely *not* saying:

I'm not saying you need to earn God's love or acceptance or approval by following all the rules and living the right kind of life. If you hear *any* version of the good news of Jesus that claims we're brought back home to God by *anything* other than the free gift of his grace—it's a scam. It's not good news at all.[7]

The question we're answering here isn't, "What do I have to do to get God to love me?"—because God's love isn't a reward to be earned; it's a gift to be received.

The question is, "How can I *experience* the truth of God's love as more than just an idea? How can I know if this stuff actually works out in real life?"

---

7 Galatians 1:6-7

And I think at least part of Jesus' answer is *by working it out in real life*.

Where the whole universe is headed

Okay. So how do we start working it out?

This is where *wisdom* comes into the picture.

And what is wisdom, exactly?

Well, remember before, when I said that love is more foundational to our universe than physics or chemistry? I wasn't talking about some vague, impersonal force; I was talking about God himself—and about the way he's set up our whole universe to run along the trajectory of his loving character.

What I mean is that, thanks to Jesus, love is where the whole universe is headed. There's no stopping it. All of history is moving in the direction of joy and peace and freedom and reconciliation. The story only ends one way: with Jesus returning to reunite heaven and earth in a perfect new creation.

In the meantime, you can either push against that reality, refusing to trust in God's love for you and trying to move off in some other direction—which, as we've seen, is what the Bible calls sin.

Or you can swim along with the current of God's love— you can move in the direction of ultimate reality— which is what the Bible calls wisdom.

Wisdom is about so much more than just information

or intelligence. Wisdom starts with knowing and loving God; it starts by approaching God with the awe and wonder and acknowledgement he deserves.[8] It's about trusting in God's love enough to live in step with reality—learning to love like he loves in all the complexity of everyday life.

Jesus himself said that all of God's wisdom for life boils down to loving God and loving others.[9] The more we live in step with the reality of God's love—the more we allow God to shape us into the kind of people who love him and love each other—the more we'll discover for ourselves that the way of Jesus really is the truest, wisest, most life-giving way to live.

Learning how to trust

This is why followers of Jesus read the Bible—not out of religious obligation, but to get to know God better, to keep learning how to trust him, and to keep figuring out how to live well in his world.[10]

And it *works*. After years of reading the Bible almost every day, I can tell you two things about this habit that are both absolutely true at the same time:

In the moment, it often feels pretty mundane.

Over the long haul, it is transforming my whole life from the inside out.

---

8 Proverbs 9:10

9 Matthew 22:36-40

10 Well, okay, plenty of Christians *do* just read the Bible out of religious obligation—but they're missing the point.

Which makes absolute sense when you think about it. Because the thing about trust—either in God, or in any other person—is that it's not a binary thing that you either 100% have or 100% *don't* have; trust grows through experience. (I'm guessing, for example, that you know and trust your best friend more fully today than you did on the day you first met.)

When it comes to God, it works like this: the more you reflect on God's wisdom and put it into practice, the more you *experience* the goodness and truth of God's wisdom. This leads you to reflect on it and practise it even more, which leads you to experience it even more, and on and on it goes—until eventually, you become "like a tree planted by streams of water", thriving and flourishing, whatever your external circumstances might be.[11]

And, listen, I'm absolutely not there yet—but I'm closer than I was a year ago, and I'm looking forward to being closer still, this time next year.

Making sense of the Bible

Of course, this isn't easy.

Some people want to tell you that the Bible is totally straightforward—all you need to do is pick it up and read it, and it should all be pretty clear to you.

I don't know about you, but that has not been my experience.

---

11 Psalm 1:1-3

The Bible contains some clear and straightforward truths; the heart of the good news—*Jesus loves me, this I know, for the Bible tells me so*—is simple enough that a tiny child can understand it. But the Bible also contains a prophet of God summoning a couple of bears to maul 42 boys for making fun of his baldness,[12] and if you think that's clear and straightforward, you and I are very different people.

The Bible is weird. It's confusing.

But it's not impossible.

And so what I want to do next is share with you five of the most helpful questions I've learned to ask as I keep figuring it all out.[13]

First, remember that the Bible is a library, not a book. Inside your Bible you'll find dozens of texts, spanning a whole range of genres and authors and purposes, which weren't gathered together into a single volume until much later. There's history, biography, poetry and songs, proverbs, parables, and a bunch of other people's mail. And so before you dive into any book of the Bible, it's helpful to step back and ask, "What kind of writing am I reading here?"

But of course, the 66 books of the Bible aren't just a random collection; the whole Bible fits together to tell one unified story that leads to Jesus. And so a second

---

12 2 Kings 2:23-25
13 These suggestions are adapted from ideas discussed in Bible Project's podcast series, The Paradigm, https://bibleproject.com/podcast/series/paradigm/ (accessed 16 Jan. 2024).

helpful question to ask about whatever part of the Bible you're reading is, "Where does this part of the Bible fit into the big story?"[14]

Third, we also need to recognise that the Bible is an ancient book, written in a vastly different culture and time to our own. We need to understand that, as the scholar John Walton so helpfully puts it, the Bible was written *for* us, but not *to* us.[15]

Yes, the Bible is God's wisdom for everyone, everywhere,[16] but God didn't just drop it out of the sky. Every part of the Bible was written by—and to—human beings living in particular times and places and cultures in the ancient world. Which means that before we can figure out what any part of the Bible means for us, we need to ask, "What did this part of the Bible mean to its original writers and readers?"

At this point, you might be thinking that this sounds like a lot of work—how are you ever meant to figure all this stuff out? Thankfully, the answer is *not all at once* and *not on your own*.

Because the next thing to keep in mind about the Bible is that it's designed to be read over and over

---

14 If you're unclear on what that big story actually is, a great starting point is Bible Project's The Story of the Bible video, which you can find here: https://bibleproject.com/explore/video/the-story-of-the-bible/. On this same website, you'll also find short videos outlining every single book of the Bible and explaining how they fit into the big story (accessed 16 Jan. 2024).

15 John H. Walton, *The Lost World of Genesis One: Ancient Cosmology and the Origins Debate* (IVP, 2009), p. 9.

16 2 Timothy 3:16-17

again for the rest of your life. You're not going to fully understand it right away because it's not *written* to be fully understood right away!

The Bible is a bottomless sea of wisdom which you can trust God to keep revealing to you bit by bit—and so rather than trying to figure out everything all at once, take the pressure off yourself and just ask, "What's something I haven't discovered before?"

And if that feels like slow going, just think of the smartest, wisest Bible nerds you know—and remember that they started out knowing less about the Bible than you do now.

Meanwhile, speaking of the Bible nerds you know, the next thing to keep in mind is that the Bible is designed to be read and figured out in community with other people. So whenever you get stuck, the fifth great question to ask yourself is, "Who can help me figure this out?"

This help might come in the form of books or podcasts or YouTube videos, but what's far more valuable and important is finding a community of actual, real, in-person people who can walk alongside you as you keep growing in the wisdom that God has for you.[17]

And above and beyond all of that, remember that it's God himself who promises to keep revealing his love and wisdom to you as you follow him—so keep on asking for his help, and keep on trusting that he couldn't be more ready to give it.[18]

---

17 Thanks for reading this book, though.
18 Matthew 7:7-12; James 1:5

Disagreeing with God

This stuff is all particularly important when we come up against stuff in the Bible that we disagree with.

What I've learned over the years is that, often, when the Bible seems to be saying something completely controversial and offensive, that's just because I haven't dug deep enough to properly understand what God is *actually* saying.

And so, rather than letting my gut reaction—*That's so disgusting and horrible!*—have the final say, I keep on investigating until I get to the point where I realise, "Oh, okay, I guess that does make sense after all".

But then, of course, there are the times when at the end of all my searching, I discover that God really *is* saying something controversial—that I've run into one of the places where our culture's view of right and wrong has diverged from Jesus' view of right and wrong.

And at that point, I have a choice:

Again, I can choose to let my gut reaction have the final say; I can assume that if something doesn't seem good or right *to me*, it can't possibly be good or right *at all*. I can decide that my wisdom is greater than God's wisdom.

Or I can choose to trust, based on everything else I know about Jesus, that he really does know better than I do. I can sit honestly with the tension of *I really don't like what the Bible is saying here*, and still choose to move forward with Jesus, guided by his wisdom, even when I don't fully get it yet—and what I've discovered is that this second choice is *always* the harder, better way.

Here's what else I've discovered as I keep on making that harder, better choice: sooner or later, as I keep growing in God's wisdom, I tend to find myself coming around to seeing things and feeling about things the way Jesus does.

But like I've been saying, it's exactly that: a discovery. It's personal. How could it be anything else when the core of the whole thing is about putting your trust in a *person*?

And so of course, as you keep going deeper—as you keep investigating and getting to know Jesus—you're inevitably going to keep running into the next thing that makes you go, "Hang on. But what about...?"

And at that point, what's so important to remember is that *your questions aren't bad*. God isn't worried or threatened by them, and you shouldn't be either. Confusion, and even doubt, are pretty standard parts of the journey; they're what you can expect to feel when you're sitting in the gap between where you are and where God wants to take you next.

The key here isn't to never doubt; it's to keep processing your doubts *with Jesus*, trusting that he's your surest guide through those dark places and back out into the light again.

I'm not telling you all this as someone who's *arrived*. I'm still on the journey of learning to trust that what God wants for me is only my deepest happiness. I'm still on the journey of aligning my wisdom with God's wisdom.

It's a rocky path—and more than a few times, I've needed Jesus to stop and pull me back up out of the ditch. But as I keep following him down the road, I know he's guiding me, step by step, into more and more of that abundant life he promises, right here in the present.

And I know he'll do the same for you.

CHAPTER 7

Who Are You Becoming?

*"We, for every kind of reason, good and bad,
are distracting ourselves into spiritual oblivion."*
—Ronald Rolheiser

Okay, so remember before, when I described wisdom as "swimming along with the current of God's love"? I should probably clarify what I *don't* mean by that.

I don't want to give you the impression that, since God's love is the direction the whole universe is headed, you can just chill back and expect to *drift* into wisdom.

Because the truth is, God's vision of reality is far from the only one on offer. We live in a world that's bombarding us with alternative visions of the good life—with all kinds of other ideas about what true wisdom looks like.

Sometimes these other ways of seeing the world are blatant and obvious—others are so subtle, we barely even notice them.

Stuck on the machine

Let me tell you something interesting that I learned about casinos a while back.

If you walked into a casino a century ago, chances are you'd find a long row of slot machines with big, pull-down handles. You put in a coin, pulled the handle—and then if everything matched up when the reels stopped spinning, a bunch of coins spilled down into the tray underneath.

But of course, technology has come a long way since then.

In the 1970s, the first video slot machines started to roll out, and they brought with them a massive, game-changing development: instead of putting in a coin and pulling down on a handle to spin the reels, you just pushed a button. Which might not sound like that big of a change—but turns out, it transformed gambling forever.

Because what do casino operators want more than anything else?

To keep you on that machine.

And what their psychologists discovered is that every time you have to reach down, pull out a coin, put it in the slot, and then reach back up and pull down on the handle, it's a great moment for your brain to pause and say, "You know what? Maybe that's enough gambling for today".

But a button takes that moment away. With a button, the movement of your body is so slight, it's barely even a conscious choice. You can just sit there in your chair going *press... press... press...* for hours and hours without even really thinking about it.

And so, with this one seemingly insignificant technological tweak, casino operators have managed to successfully hack the brains of millions of people.

I heard one casino worker describe how every night after their shift, there'd be a row of slot-machine seats waiting outside to be cleaned because they'd been soiled by gamblers who'd been so in the zone, they hadn't even got up to go to the toilet.[1]

And this explains why it's so easy for you to pick up your phone for a minute and then look up and wonder how half an hour's gone by already—because the *exact same* technology and psychology that casino operators use to keep gamblers hooked on their machines is being used by social media companies to keep us hooked on our phones.

Once upon a time, the internet was mostly divided up into pages. You scrolled down a page, hit the bottom—and then you had to stop and make a decision about where you were going to click next. This moment of

---

1 Your Undivided Attention: What Happened in Vegas—with Natasha Dow Schüll (https://podcasts.apple.com/au/podcast/your-undivided-attention/id1460030305?i=1000441077287), accessed 16 Jan. 2024.

decision was the equivalent of reaching for the pull-down handle on that old slot machine: it gave your brain a moment to pause and say, "Maybe that's enough internet for today".

But then a programmer named Aza Raskin invented the infinite scroll, which is how we experience social media today. Thanks to this new innovation, there's no such thing as the bottom of the page anymore.

Just like the casinos, our social media platforms have successfully eliminated any logical end-point to your experience—with the result that you just sit there on your bed going *swipe... swipe... swipe...* without even thinking about it, and before you know it, you've used up half your whole afternoon.

One day, Raskin got curious about just how much extra time people were spending on social media thanks to his invention. If he started with the lowball estimate that infinite scroll makes you spend 50% more time online, and then multiplied that out by the billions of people using social media every day, where did the numbers land?

The answer he came up with was staggering: every single day "the combined total of 200,000 more total human lifetimes—every moment from birth to death—is now spent scrolling through a screen".[2]

---

2 Hari, *Stolen Focus*, p. 115-116.

The things we do, do something to us

Why am I telling you all this?

Well, you know how I said earlier that a regular Bible-reading habit, even though it might seem pretty inconsequential in the moment, can be life-transforming over the long haul? The exact same thing is true of social media—or whatever else we consistently give our attention to.

There's this concept in brain science called neuroplasticity, which describes the way our minds are shaped by our behaviour. Your brain is not a static object; it's constantly rewiring itself. Neurons in your brain that repeatedly activate in particular patterns are more likely to fire in those *same* patterns the next time they're activated. What this means is that the more you repeat an action, a behaviour, or a thought pattern, the more natural that repetition becomes.

To put it another way: "The things we do, *do something to us*. They shape the people we become."[3]

Which means that our capacity to pursue wisdom—to pursue the deep riches of life and joy that Jesus has for us—is *deeply* tied to our habits. If we want to grow in wisdom, we need to choose habits that are going to help us stay engaged and thoughtful. We need habits that are going to keep aligning our hearts and minds and choices with the reality of God's love and goodness—with *how things really are*.

---

3 John Mark Comer, *Live No Lies: Recognize and Resist the Three Enemies That Sabotage Your Peace* (Waterbrook Press, 2021), p. 169.

Social media shapes our minds in the *opposite* direction: not towards active, thoughtful choices, but towards endless passive engagement. The algorithms driving these platforms aren't calibrated to bring you truth, or even enjoyment; they're designed to keep you in the zone.

The reason why social media companies don't charge you anything is that you aren't the customer—you're the product. The real customers are the companies who advertise on these platforms. What's being sold is your attention.[4]

Which is a massive problem for those of us who are trying to follow Jesus into the lives we were actually created for.

Because, for better or worse, what we give our attention to shapes who we become—and the more time we spend on social media, the more we're surrendering our freedom to *choose* what we give our attention to. We're deciding to let the algorithms choose for us.[5]

The illusory truth effect

This is all exacerbated by what psychologists call the *illusory truth effect*.

Remember, the more often something repeats in your brain, the more natural and automatic each repetition

---

4 Seth Godin, "When Your Phone Uses You", https://seths. blog/2016/12/when-your-phone-uses-you/ (accessed 17 Jan. 2024).

5 I tell you all this as someone who stayed up too late last night, scrolling on Instagram. I don't have this stuff nailed yet either.

becomes—and it turns out this isn't just true about habits; it's also true about *ideas*.

Your brain finds it easier to process an old idea—one it's already encountered before—than a new one. As a result, the more often an idea is repeated to you, the more likely your brain is to accept that idea, regardless of whether it's *actually* true or not.

(The point here is not that our brains *can't* find the truth; it's to say that what intuitively *feels* true and what *is* true are not always the same thing.)

Combine the illusory truth effect with an addictive social media algorithm and you have a recipe for disaster, because every video you watch is making some kind of claim about what's true—and the more we scroll, the more compelling these claims become, regardless of whether or not they reflect actual reality.

If we're not careful, we'll end up being influenced far more by the values of our wider culture than the values of Jesus, not because we've consciously decided our culture's voice is more true or trustworthy, but just because *we become what we give our attention to*.

The renewing of your mind

Obviously, this is not just a social media issue. It's not even a *new* issue.

Two thousand years ago, Jesus described a kind of person who hears the good news he came to bring and who maybe even *believes* it intellectually—"but as they go on their way they are choked by life's worries, riches and pleasures, and they do not mature".[6]

Why do these people miss out on the fullness of life that God has for them?

It's not because they're busy doing terrible things.

They're just *distracted*.

Instead of fixing their attention on Jesus and letting *him* transform them into people who are more like him, they're letting their attention drift towards other things, and being transformed in *that* direction instead—and as a result, they miss out on the best God has for them.

So how do we avoid making the same mistake?

One early follower of Jesus wrote this to his fellow Christians: "Do not conform to the pattern of this world, but *be transformed by the renewing of your mind*. Then you will be able to test and approve what God's will is—his good, pleasing and perfect will."[7]

The renewing of our minds is God's work in us—but it's a work he wants us to participate in. And as far as I can see, the most effective way to partner with God in the renewing of our *minds* is by renewing our *focus*.

I'm not saying to throw away your phone—but if you're spending five minutes each day focusing on God and five hours each day scrolling on your phone, it probably

---

6   Luke 8:14
7   Romans 12:2, emphasis mine.

shouldn't surprise you if God feels distant. You're literally *rewiring your brain* to feel that way.

On the other hand, if you deliberately create space in your life to return your attention to the deepest truth in the universe—to God, and his abundant love for you—it won't be long before you feel your heart and mind transforming in *that* direction.

And the good news is, Jesus has already shown us how it's done.

How Jesus did it

As you read through the biographies of Jesus, you'll notice a set of habits that he practised over and over again.

The first one is that "Jesus often withdrew to lonely places and prayed".[8] No matter what else he had going on (and I think it's safe to say Jesus had some pretty significant demands on his time), he regularly made time to go off by himself and focus his attention on God his Father—to talk to him, and to let him set the trajectory of the rest of his day.

The second habit is being so deeply immersed in his Bible—what we now call the Old Testament—that, no matter what situation he faced, he *always* had some bit of wisdom from the Scriptures to guide what he said and did.[9]

---

8 Luke 5:16
9 At this point you may be thinking, "Well, yeah, but of course Jesus knew the Bible back to front—Jesus is God". And sure, that's true.

Another thing you'll notice is how *deeply* committed Jesus was to living his life in community. He surrounded himself with close friends, he regularly went to the synagogue to worship with God's people, and he spent so much time at parties that he was falsely accused of being a glutton and a drunk.[10] Time alone with God was deeply important to Jesus—but so was time together with others.

Now, at this point you may be experiencing a sinking feeling—because you may have noticed that what I'm talking about here basically boils down to, *pray, read the Bible and go to church*. Which you might think is the exact same stuff that hasn't seemed to make much positive difference to your life in the past.

And, look, I get it. Like I've said already, this stuff often feels mundane and uninspiring before it feels transformative. But if you stick with it, God *will* use these habits to transform you.

In my experience, the key is to just *keep showing up*—on the days when you feel like it, and especially on the days when you really don't—and *keep leaning in*, trusting that God is at work through it all, even when you can't see it happening.

But Jesus is also fully human. He didn't just get the Scriptures downloaded into his brain at birth. In his human life on earth, Jesus got to know the Bible the same way you can: by investing regular time in reading or listening to it.

10   Matthew 11:19

Putting it into practice

Here's what this looks like for me.[11]

First thing in the morning—*before* I look at my phone—I aim to get out of bed early enough to spend 20 minutes or so alone in the quiet.

I sit down with a cup of coffee and just stare out the window for a bit.

I focus my attention on God, and then get distracted, and then focus my attention on God again.

I let him remind me of what's been true all along: that he's with me, that he loves me, and that whatever the day ahead might hold, he's ready and waiting to help me through it.

I pray for a bit.

I read or listen to the next chapter of one of the Gospels.

I might grab my journal and write down an idea that jumps out to me, or a few things I'm grateful for.

And then I get on with my day—and, more often than not, get drawn into the same busyness and distraction that everyone else does.

And so the thing I'm most intentionally working on these days is what one writer called *practising the presence of God*,[12] which basically just looks like bringing my

---

11 Obviously, there are plenty of times when the wheels fall off and my day doesn't work out like this—but these are the habits I'm aiming for when I get up in the morning.

12 Brother Lawrence, *The Practice of the Presence of God.*

focus back to God, as often as I can remember to do it throughout the day—asking him to keep reminding me of his love, and to keep showing me the next way he's inviting me to share that love with the people around me.

And speaking of the people around me, I also make it a priority to show up to my church gathering every Sunday—and to set aside time throughout the week to spend with other followers of Jesus. (I'll talk more in Chapter 9 about why this is such a big deal, but for now let me just make the point that *following Jesus with other people* isn't just *a great* way to do it; it's *the* way to do it.)

The person you're becoming

Remember, the point of all this isn't to *do more good Christian things*.

The point is the person you're becoming.

The Bible uses the language of Jesus being formed *in* us[13]—of a complete, caterpillar-to-butterfly-level transformation of your life into the image of Jesus.

Which, obviously, is not going to be a speedy, straight-line experience.

You, like the rest of us, are going to mess this up all the time.

There will be these bright, shimmering moments along the way when people are going to look at you, and it's going to be like catching a glimpse of Jesus himself.

---

13 Galatians 4:19

And then there'll be the other moments.

The moments when you fail to believe that what God wants for you is only your deepest happiness, when you lose sight of the reality that living to please God is the only true path to your deepest joy and flourishing. The moments when life's worries, riches, and pleasures lead you astray, and you wake up in the morning and feel the weight of what you did yesterday come crashing down on you.

And it's those moments when you *most* need to remember that *it's all grace*—God's free gift, from beginning to end.[14]

So just keep turning back to Jesus. Come to him with whatever's burdening you—with all the ways you've messed up—and ask for his forgiveness, and rejoice in the knowledge that he's already taken care of *all of it* on the cross.

And then *keep moving forward with Jesus,* remembering that all you've ever been doing here is partnering with God in *his* work—and trusting in the promise that "he who began a good work in you *will* carry it on to completion until the day of Christ Jesus."[15]

---

14 Ephesians 2:8-9
15 Philippians 1:6, emphasis mine.

CHAPTER 8

Disappointment and Disaster

"The last enemy to be destroyed is death."
—1 Corinthians 15:26

One of the most important—and absolute worst—parts of my work as a school chaplain, and also of being so deeply involved in my local church community, is that I end up going to far more funerals than normal people do.

Some of these funerals are kind of okay—the ones where the person has lived a rich, full life and passed away peacefully in their sleep, surrounded by friends and family. Those deaths are still heartbreaking, obviously, but to me at least, they're the easiest to make sense of.

It's the other ones that get to me. Funerals for my work friends or their family members who have died way too young—from long, drawn-out illnesses, or tragic, out-of-the-blue accidents.

Funerals for kids who have lost their lives, sometimes after an ongoing struggle with disease, and sometimes with no concrete medical explanation at all.

Funerals for young mothers and fathers.

I've stood with little children weeping over the coffins of their parents, and parents weeping over the coffins of their little children.

More times than I can count, I've sat and cried and prayed with people in the midst of the deepest heartache that life can throw at you. And the truth is, getting to walk alongside the people I care about through some of the darkest moments of their lives is a profound privilege. I wouldn't trade it for the world.

But it's also *awful*.

And what makes it all the more difficult to make sense of is that many of these people's families were up through the night praying for them, begging God to keep the one they loved from dying.

And the one they loved still died.

Two different directions

When I talk to my friends who have walked away from following Jesus—who have given up on trusting in God's love for them—one theme that comes up over and over again is their experience of suffering and tragedy.

Because if God really is all-powerful, and if he really is all-loving—if he's strong and kind enough to stop their pain and heartbreak anytime he wants, or to prevent it from ever happening in the first place, then why in the world doesn't he?

It feels like a betrayal, like needless cruelty.

And so they come to the conclusion that God isn't worth putting their trust in, or that he was never even there in the first place, and they give up on the whole thing.

To be honest, I can see where they're coming from—but what's so interesting to me is that things can also run in the complete opposite direction.

Because when I talk to my friends who are most *deeply* committed to following Jesus—who most confidently trust in God's love for them—one theme that comes up over and over again is *their* experience of suffering and tragedy, and how it deepened their faith.

So how do we explain that? Why does the pain and brokenness of the world drive some people further away from Jesus and draw other people closer to him?

A problem for the heart

On an intellectual level, the "How could a good God let me keep suffering?" question has a pretty straightforward answer:

> "If you have a God great and transcendent enough to
> be mad at because he hasn't stopped evil and suffering
> in the world, then you have (at the same moment)

*a God great and transcendent enough to have good
reasons for allowing it to continue that you can't
know. Indeed, you can't have it both ways."*[1]

In other words, just because we can't see a good reason
for God to allow our suffering to continue, that doesn't
mean there isn't one. Which, if we were just machines
calculating the data and spitting out the most logical
answer, would be all well and good.

But of course, we're not just machines. And suffering
isn't just a problem for the head; it's a problem for the
heart—a problem that cuts right to the core of our all-
important question:

Can I trust him?

Why rejecting God doesn't help

Let's start with the obvious: suffering is a part of life.

I assume you already know that all too well from first-
hand experience—and if not, I hate to break it to you,
but you will soon enough.

And even if you, like me, have mostly had a pretty
privileged, comfortable life so far, you're still surrounded
by other people's suffering, whether that's your own
close people, or just out there in the wider world.

Jesus was very up-front about all this. He said, "In this
world *you will have trouble*".[2]

---

1   Timothy Keller, *The Reason for God: Belief in an Age of Scepticism*, p. 25.
2   John 16:33, emphasis mine.

And so, for all of us, the question isn't, *Will trouble come my way?*

It's, *Where will I turn when it does?*

And while it's easy to see how suffering can lead to confusion and disillusionment and disappointment with God, the truth is, deleting him from the equation isn't going to take your pain away.

If anything, it's going to do the opposite.

Because if there's no God, if your suffering isn't part of some bigger story he's telling, if we're all just here by accident, then here's what's true about your pain... there's no ultimate value or meaning to it, because *existence* has no ultimate value or meaning.

There's no guarantee that things will ever turn around or get better—and even if things *do* somehow happen to get better for a while, you're still faced with the inevitable and permanent reality of death.

Whatever happens in the meantime, one day you will die and be forgotten, and so will everyone you love, along with every last one of their grandchildren and great-grandchildren.

Eventually, our sun will grow old and die, and so will all the other suns. Until at last, our ever-expanding universe will hit what scientists call "maximum entropy"—by which point, it will be unable to support life of any kind.

The last star will go out, the last organism will die, and there'll be no one left to remember anything.

The end.

If there's no God, then your suffering is just one more meaningless drop in the vast ocean that will one day drown the whole cosmos.

And so, as impossible as it might feel to keep trusting God in the middle of your pain and suffering, the truth is, it's hard to see how cutting him out of the picture really gets you anywhere.

But, alright, so let's say we bring God back into the picture. How does that help us?

Our help in trouble

There's a poem in the Bible that begins with these words: "God is our refuge and strength, an ever-present help in trouble."[3]

Notice that word "in".

There are plenty of places in the Bible where we see God protecting his people *from* trouble—and whenever we experience that in our own lives we should, of course, rejoice and be grateful—but that's not the promise here.

The promise is that God will be with us *in* the trouble, and that he'll lead us safely through to the other side.

"Therefore," the poem continues, "we will not fear, though the earth give way, and the mountains fall into the heart of the sea".[4]

---

3 Psalm 46:1
4 Psalm 46:2

The "sea" in the ancient world was a symbol of chaos, disorder and instability—and so, needless to say, if the mountain you're standing on is crumbling into the sea, you are not having your best day.

Even so, the poet insists, there's no need to be afraid. Instead, we should drag our focus away from our fears and fix it back onto God, letting the Lord remind us again of the truth about his loving character.

"Be still," he says, "and know that I am God".[5]

Which would be a whole lot harder for me to get my head around if God hadn't already painted us a vivid picture of exactly who he is.

God's truest, best answer

In the end, God's truest, best, most complete answer to all our questions about our suffering is not an argument; it's a person.[6]

It's God himself, here on earth as Jesus.

Over and over again through Jesus' life, we see God's overflowing compassion for the lost, the broken and the grieving. We see him feeding the hungry, welcoming the lonely, healing the sick, raising the dead—and weeping with those who weep.

Jesus shows us that God is *with us* in our suffering. I don't just mean that he comes alongside us while *we*

---

5 Psalm 46:10

6 Full credit to Timothy Keller for being the first person I ever heard explain it like this.

suffer, although that's absolutely true; what I mean is that Jesus has suffered too.

In Jesus, God has fully entered into the human experience. In Jesus, the one who holds the whole universe together knows what it's like to go through illness, injury, suffering, heartache and tragedy. He's been betrayed by his friends, whispered about behind his back, misunderstood by accident and misunderstood on purpose. He's had long days and sleepless nights.

In Jesus, God knows what it's like to die.

But he also knows what it's like to come back to life.

Take heart

I don't know the reason for your suffering—and to be honest, I doubt knowing the "reason" for it would make much difference to the pain, anyway.

But all you need to do is look at Jesus' death to know that, whatever the reason is, it's not that God doesn't get it, or that he doesn't care.

And all you need to do is look at Jesus' resurrection to know that, whatever the reason is, it's not that God isn't strong enough to deal with your situation.

"In this world you will have trouble," Jesus said. "But take heart! I have overcome the world."[7]

Through his death and resurrection, Jesus has conquered death itself. Which means that as you put your trust in

7 John 16:33

him, here's what you *can* know about your suffering with absolute certainty:

It's temporary.

The day is coming when Jesus will return to take all of our pain and suffering and cast it out into the cosmic garbage dump. Which means that, here and now, by faith in Jesus, you can look at *any* situation, no matter how broken, and say, "This is *not okay*—but it will be".

If the story isn't good, that just means the story isn't over yet.

The God of all comfort

In the meantime, God has not left us on our own.

He's our refuge and strength, our ever-present help in trouble.

And as we keep holding on to the great hope we have in Jesus, he promises to take all the circumstances of our lives—even the absolute worst of them—and weave them into the fabric of the vast, eternal story of rescue and redemption he's telling.

Which is not to say that our pain really isn't so bad after all—but that God is just too good to let any of it go to waste. He promises to use our pain and suffering to grow us and transform us—to make us more like Jesus himself.[8]

In the meantime, we can process our fear and doubt

---

8 Romans 5:3-5; James 1:2-4

and disappointment and frustration with God—which, again, brings us back to prayer.

Through prayer, we come before the throne of the universe, knowing that, as we do, we're coming before our gracious Father who loves us, and who is powerful to help.

Which, like I've been saying, is not a promise that things will always go our way; for as long as Jesus waits to return, suffering is going to be part of the picture.[9]

And so maybe God will answer your prayer by miraculously taking away the obstacles in front of you—or maybe he'll answer your prayer by seeing you *through* your situation and out the other side. But either way, you can count on him to hear your cry for help, and to respond with love and compassion.

And as you do that, you can rest assured that, whatever you're going through, you are not alone. Your situation is not hopeless, and it's not permanent.

Our great God of love—"the Father of compassion and the God of all comfort"[10]—is still on the throne.

You can trust him.

---

9 And remember, the reason Jesus is waiting is so more people can be part of the new creation: "The Lord is not slow in keeping his promise, as some understand slowness. Instead he is patient with you, not wanting anyone to perish, but everyone to come to repentance" (2 Peter 3:9).

10 2 Corinthians 1:3

CHAPTER 9

How to Change the World

"You can't follow Jesus alone. Not 'shouldn't'. Can't."
—*John Mark Comer*

So far, we've been focusing a lot on the difference that Jesus can make to your *internal* world—on how trusting and following Jesus can reshape your life on the inside. Which, in our post-Christian cultural moment in history, is generally pretty socially acceptable.

If you're into Jesus the same way other people are into mindfulness or horoscopes or going to the gym—if you're taking Jesus on as part of your own personal self-improvement journey—most people's attitude is, *Well, I might think it's a little weird, but who am I to judge? You do you. Just don't take it too seriously, and don't tell me I have to join you.*

Personal faith is mostly still welcome in our post-Christian culture, as long as you keep it to yourself. But when you start expressing your beliefs in public—when you start talking about Jesus' teachings like they're not just *opinions* but the *truth*—that's when people get a whole lot less comfortable. People can start to see you as coercive, intolerant or even threatening.[1]

Which, as followers of Jesus, puts us in a tough spot—because the claims Jesus went around making while he was here on earth weren't just claims about personal spirituality; they were declarations about *reality itself.*

"The time has come," he said. "The kingdom of God has come near. Repent and believe the good news!"[2]

The good news of Jesus isn't just good news about you and your personal situation (although, of course, it includes that.) It's good news about a kingdom that's coming to transform the whole universe.

And Jesus' declaration to everyone, everywhere is that the *only* fitting response to this good news is to "repent": to turn around—to change your mind and to change your direction.

Jesus' message isn't, *I've come to offer you my personal perspective so that you can consider whether it's a good fit for your life.*

---

1 Tyson and Grizzle, *A Creative Minority*, p. 9.
2 Mark 1:15

Jesus' message is, *I've come to show you the ultimate truth about reality so that you can start living in step with how things really are. This is where the whole universe is headed. Are you getting on board or not?*

Which, of course, hits the ears of our post-Christian culture as being impossibly intolerant and exclusive.

But if Jesus really is who he says he is, then these claims aren't just his personal opinions; they're *true*.

Living out of step with reality

Let's say a friend you deeply love comes to the conclusion that gravity doesn't exist. They get lost down a late-night internet rabbit hole, watch a bunch of gravity truther videos, and come out the other side believing that gravity is just a vast conspiracy cooked up by a global cabal of airline companies to sell you plane tickets.

You might say your friend is entitled to their opinion—people have a right to believe whatever they want—but if you catch your friend halfway out of a fourth-floor window with cardboard wings strapped to their arms, you're still going to try to talk them back from the edge, right?

Because your friend is living out of step with reality. Because there's a path that leads to your friend's true joy and flourishing—not to mention survival—and this isn't it. Urging your friend to repent—to change their mind and change their direction—isn't intolerant or narrow-minded in this situation.

Yes, you're making an exclusive claim. You're saying, "My understanding of gravity is truer to reality than your understanding of gravity, and I think you should change your mind". But under the circumstances, this is the most loving thing you could possibly do.

And this is what Jesus is doing when he calls us to turn around and follow him. He's being exclusive and narrow and *absolutely loving*—because he's leading us back to reality.

An uncomfortable tension

But, like I said, this puts followers of Jesus in a strange position.

Because the thing about gravity is it's pretty uncontroversial. It has massive implications for your day-to-day life, but no one thinks you're weird or offensive for letting your beliefs about gravity shape your thinking or your behaviour.

Jesus is different—no less significant, but a whole lot more controversial.

Jesus invites us into a whole new way of life where every part of who we are, how we think, and how we live is brought into line with his vision of reality.

Following Jesus will mean rethinking where we devote our money, time, and attention; reshaping how we understand our bodies, our sexuality, and our gender identity; reimagining how we approach pressing global issues and how we treat the person right in front of us.

Again, this isn't about getting in line with some arbitrary list of rules or standards, but about walking in step with the perfect love of God—with *how things really are*.

But of course, not everyone agrees that this is how things really are.

And so we live with this uncomfortable tension: we believe that the gospel really is the best news the world has ever known—that the hope and healing and abundant life our friends are crying out for is a gift that Jesus has already died to bring them. At the same time, we feel misunderstood and seen as backwards, prejudiced religious hypocrites. We want to bring the hope of Jesus to the world, to bring positive change, but we don't know how to do it.[3]

So if the good news of Jesus really is the best news the world has ever known, what does it look like to *live out* that good news, and to share it with the people around us, who may see things very differently?

How should we, as followers of Jesus, engage with our post-Christian culture?

Option 1: Retreat

Some people's solution is to *retreat* from culture—to withdraw into a safe Christian bubble and just kind of hang in there until Jesus comes back. They spend their lives hanging out with other Christians, listening to Christian music, watching Christian movies, and

---

3   Tyson and Grizzle, *A Creative Minority*, p. 50.

following Christian influencers on social media.

They still believe in the importance of sharing the good news of Jesus, but this mostly looks like faithfully preaching that good news from inside their safe Christian spaces, and praying that other people will come and join them.

And, of course, it's not that all of this is wrong; it's just incomplete.

Jesus told his followers to go out into the whole world and share the good news, to keep pursuing his mission to find God's lost children and bring them home—not to just stay inside and hope they find their way home on their own.[4]

Option 2: Control

Other people's approach is to try to *control* the culture. They look at the influence that Christians used to have in Western society, and they think, "We need to get that back".

And so, through political power and social activism, they try to steer the culture back on track by protesting what they believe is wrong and by campaigning for new laws that they hope will make society look more like how they think Jesus would want it to look.

One major danger with this approach is that, to the people around us, it can often feel less like we're bringing good news and more like we're just trying to force them

---

4 Matthew 28:18-20; Acts 1:8; Luke 19:10

to live according to a set of values they don't believe in.[5] It can seem less like love for others and more like fighting for our own rights and comfort—and if that's what we're doing, we've missed the mark entirely.[6]

Because the way of Jesus isn't about us transforming people's behaviour from the outside in; it's about Jesus transforming their hearts from the inside out.

Of course, there's plenty of good and important work to be done through healthy political engagement. But at the end of the day, your political power is really not all that crucial to Jesus' plans, because he's already the King of the universe. He's going to keep on growing his kingdom, no matter who's running your country or what laws they've put in place.

Option 3: Compromise

A third option is to *compromise* with the culture—to hold on to the values of Jesus that our post-Christian society still agrees with, and to let go of the ones that have become socially unacceptable.

But in the end, this isn't following Jesus at all. It's following the culture, and letting Jesus come along for the ride if he agrees to behave himself.

Option 4: The way of Jesus

Thankfully, there's a better way. It's the same way that Jesus called his first disciples to live in the world, and

---

5   Tyson and Grizzle, *A Creative Minority*, p. 9-10.

6   1 Corinthians 10:24; Philippians 2:4; Galatians 6:10

it's just as simple, beautiful and earth-shattering today as it was back then:

A new command I give you: love one another. As I have loved you, so you must love one another. By this everyone will know that you are my disciples, if you love one another.[7]

How do we respond to our culture when it disagrees with us? How do we show the world who Jesus really is? How do we participate with him in the renewal and restoration of the whole universe?

We love each other with the love of Jesus.

Which might seem overly simplistic—even a little bit naive—but after Jesus rose from the dead and returned to heaven, his first followers put his words to the test—and it turned the whole world upside down.

As far as most people around them were concerned, the Jesus movement was irrelevant at best, and offensive and dangerous at worst. Why would anyone keep following Jesus when his death had already proven he was just one more failed, would-be revolutionary?

But Jesus' followers just kept right on following him. They kept on insisting that he really had risen from the dead, and they kept on living their lives together as if they really did believe God's love was the most powerful force in the universe.

They loved their enemies and forgave their persecutors.

---

7 John 13:34-35

They practised radical generosity and hospitality. They clothed the poor and cared for the sick. They ate together and made sure no one went hungry. They demolished the barriers between men and women, rich and poor, slaves and masters. They pushed back against the brutality of life under Roman rule with the love and compassion of Jesus. No one had ever seen anything like it.[8]

And as people on the outside watched all this happening—as they felt their doubts about Jesus slip away in the face of the miracle they were seeing right in front of them—Jesus' followers welcomed them in with open arms and said, "You're invited too!"

And so the Jesus movement continued to grow, until it transformed first the Roman Empire and then the whole world, not through violence or coercion but by living a better story.

Your family needs you

Today we are, once again, living in an era where many people consider the Jesus movement to be irrelevant at best, and offensive and dangerous at worst—and the truth is, they're probably not going to start trusting in the love of Jesus just because we *tell* them about it.

They need to experience it for themselves.

They need to *see* the miracle of Jesus' love lived out in front of them.

---

8 Michael Frost, *Surprise the World: The Five Habits of Highly Missional People* (NavPress, 2015), p. 7-8.

And the only way we can make that happen is *together*.

This is why church is so important. And when I say "church", I don't mean the church *building*, or even church *services*. I mean the *family* of Jesus' people, loving one another and welcoming the world to join us.

Don't get me wrong, meeting together each week as a local church community to pray and worship and learn from the Bible together is incredibly valuable and important. Get involved. Stay involved. (And by that, I mean *actually involved*. Pray along with prayers, read along in your Bible, take notes, ask questions, sing like you mean it—because the more you join in, the more you'll get out of it.)

But whatever you do, don't stop there—because Jesus didn't die and rise again just so you could be adopted into a church service; he did it so you could be adopted into a *family*.

That family needs you, and you need them—not just for an hour or two a week but through all the ups and downs of your lives together—in order to learn from one another, to encourage one another, to remind each other that you're not crazy, to keep spurring one another on[9]—and, through it all, to *show* the love of Jesus to the watching world.

So where might you start? What might it look like to take the next step deeper into community with Jesus' people? Who from your church family can you text or

---

9 Hebrews 10:23-25

call to check in on? Who can you organise to hang out with on the weekend? Who can you meet up to pray with? Who can you talk to about that question about God or life or the Bible that's been nagging at you?

Why not take a moment, even right now, to stop and ask God to point someone out to you? See who he brings to mind, and then reach out and take the next step.

If your local church community happens to be full of people you have tons in common with, this will all feel a bit easier and more straightforward. But even if it doesn't—even if you're the only one your age or if no one else there is into the same stuff you are—just push through the awkwardness and dive in anyway. Because what you *do* have in common is Jesus, and that's so much more important than anything else.

Your church—your local gathering of Jesus' family, however flawed and unimpressive they might seem—is a gift from God to you, as you are to them. You can trust him to keep on growing you up together into more and more of the love of Jesus.

And together, for all our flaws, we also have the incredible opportunity to be a gift from God to the people around us. As we live together in community, sharing God's love and pursuing God's wisdom, we can trust him to keep working through us, to paint a picture for the watching world of what Jesus' love is really like.

CHAPTER 10

How to Live with Your Family

"It is easy to love the people far away. It is not always easy to love those close to us."
—Mother Theresa

There's a moment that happens like clockwork, every single year in my fifth-grade Christian Studies classes at school.

I show the class these words from Jesus:

You have heard that it was said, "Love your neighbour and hate your enemy." But I tell you, love your enemies and pray for those who persecute you, that you may be children of your Father in heaven.[1]

---

1 Matthew 5:43-45

And then I ask my students a few questions:

"What do we think about this idea of loving our neighbours—of loving the people around us?"

At this point, I can usually count on a general murmur of agreement.

"Okay, and what do we think about the idea of loving even our enemies?"

Here, we might run into some questions, but I can generally count on the class to at least kind of agree that loving your enemies is, in theory, a good thing to do.

"Alright, so, next question: what if I told you that loving your neighbours and your enemies also includes loving your own siblings?"

At this point, there is immediate rioting. Kids start flipping over tables, smashing their chairs through the windows, setting fire to the carpet, running screaming from the room.

Well, okay, slight exaggeration. But I can always count on my students' immediate, visceral resistance to this idea.

Loving and forgiving a serial axe-murderer?

Sure, why not?

Loving and forgiving my *sister*?

Nope. No can do.

Which actually makes perfect sense when you think

about it. Loving a theoretical murderer is easy, because you only need to do it in your imagination. Loving your brother or sister is way harder, because they're right there in front of you, being obnoxious.

Jesus' teaching about love is easy to get on board with as a beautiful ideal. But the closer you are to someone—especially, I think, to someone you didn't choose to be this close to—the more they put your capacity for love to the test. And for most of us, no one fits this description better than family.

However well you get on with your family, there are still going to be moments when it's hard to love them (and, let's face it, when it's hard for them to love us).

So what do we do about that?

What Jesus means by "love"

The first thing to say here is that when Jesus talks about love, he's not mostly talking about your feelings.

We tend to think of love mainly as a feeling that happens *to* us—but Jesus has a different definition. For Jesus, love is *action*; it's putting the other person first.[2] And the other person doesn't only include people you find it easy to get along with; for Jesus, the ultimate standard of authentic love is how well you treat the person you can't stand.[3]

---

2 John 13:1-17; Philippians 2:3

3 Matthew 5:43-48; Luke 10:25-37. See also Bible Project, "Agape/ Love", https://bibleproject.com/explore/video/agape-love/ (accessed 24 Jan. 2024).

Which, strangely enough, suddenly seems way more achievable to me.

Because if Jesus is telling me to feel warm, fuzzy feelings for my sister even when she's being a total pain, then I don't even know where to start.

But if Jesus is telling me to just go ahead and take the most loving action—to do what's best for the other person, even when I'm *not* feeling it—then that's a choice I actually have some control over.

It's not easy, but it's possible.

And don't forget what we saw back in chapter 7 about how our habits shape the people we're becoming. As you keep asking for God's help to practise loving *action*—to let the other person have the better seat, or the bigger bit of dessert, or the first shower, or the last word—you can trust him to keep growing you up into the kind of person whose actions *and* feelings line up more and more closely with his own perfect love.

And of course, you can count on your family to give you *plenty* of opportunities to practise.

Tear up the scorecard

There's this famous moment when Jesus' friend Peter came up to him with a question: "Lord, how many times shall I forgive my brother or sister who sins against me? Up to seven times?"[4]

---

4 Matthew 18:21. Peter isn't asking specifically about literal siblings here, but Jesus' wisdom about forgiveness applies to them too.

The general wisdom in their culture was that three times was enough to show that you had a forgiving heart—and so, by throwing out *seven* times as an option, I think Peter imagined himself as being extremely generous here.

But Jesus' response blew both those numbers out of the water: "I tell you, not seven times, but seventy-seven times."[5]

Actually, some translators argue that what Jesus actually said was, "seventy *times* seven times".

And if you're thinking, *But by then I would have lost count*, I think that's exactly Jesus' point. He's not saying that you should forgive until you hit 77 (or 490) on your scorecard, and then kick your brother or sister to the curb.

He's saying, *Tear up the scorecard and throw it away.*

Keep choosing love and forgiveness, even after you've lost count of how many times you've had to do it. In fact, if you're still keeping score of all the ways your brother or sister (or whoever) has wronged you, chances are you haven't *actually* forgiven them at all.

Now, of course, none of this means you should just let another person keep hurting you—if you need help with a situation, reach out and find it—but whatever else you do, keep choosing to act with love, because that's exactly how Jesus treats you.

---

5 Matthew 18:22

At the cross, Jesus tore up your scorecard and threw it away.

How can we, as his people, do anything else?

Obviously, none of this is easy. In fact, the kind of deep, lasting forgiveness that Jesus talks about here is impossible for you to achieve on your own. Thankfully, Jesus is right there with you, absolutely committed to helping you walk it out.

Meanwhile, if the prospect of forgiving someone 490 times still just feels exhausting to you, the good news is, you never *actually* have to forgive them hundreds of times.

You only ever have to forgive them *this time*.

If someone wrongs you, just ask for God's help to forgive them once.

And if they do it again, ask for God's help to forgive them once—again.

Sure, sooner or later, those times will all add up, but don't focus on that because you'll just get overwhelmed. Instead, just focus on forgiving them *this* time, and trust God's Spirit to meet you with the strength you need to forgive them next time, whenever that next time might be.

A quiet revolution

When my sister and I were teenagers, we used to fight *constantly*. We were horrible to each other. If you had told me that we'd end up being best friends one day, I would have told you it was impossible.

Thankfully, impossible is no problem for Jesus.

My parents are both followers of Jesus, and so my sister and I grew up going to church and reading the Bible and praying—but it wasn't until I was around 15 years old that my faith really went from something my family believed to something I intentionally took on for myself.

And to me, it didn't really seem like anything much had changed.

But to my sister, it was a quiet revolution.

"Are you kidding?" she said years later when I asked her about it. "Of course I could tell the difference! You finally stopped being so mean to me all the time!"

Don't get me wrong; it wasn't as though I'd been magically transformed overnight or anything.

But as I grew in my faith, I guess I just started taking more responsibility for my half of our relationship—which, over time, ended up making a huge difference to our relationship overall—until one day, we both looked up and realised we actually kind of liked hanging out with each other.

What about my parents?

When it comes to your relationship with your parents (or whatever other adults are part of your household), there's obviously a very different set of dynamics at play. Everything I've talked about so far still applies—but with your parents, there's the added factor that they're the ones in charge.

Which doesn't *have* to be terrible. In fact, the Bible lays out a really beautiful vision of how it's supposed to work. (This vision assumes a household full of people that are following Jesus. If that's not your situation, hang in there; we'll get to that next.)

The Bible's vision for family life starts with the assumption that everyone in the household—children, parents, grandparents, whoever—is choosing to "submit to one another out of reverence for Christ".[6] They're choosing to live as Jesus lived: not looking to their own interests, but each person looking to the interests of the others.[7]

With that in mind, children are called to demonstrate the love of Jesus by honouring and obeying their parents—and parents are called to demonstrate the love of Jesus by not infuriating their children, and by seeking to be the kind of parents whose wisdom and instruction is *worth* obeying.[8]

Which is great when everyone's doing their part, loving each other and putting each other first. But of course, we don't always (or even often) live up to this ideal.

But just because your family, like everyone else's, is flawed, that doesn't mean Jesus or his teaching are.

---

6 Ephesians 5:21
7 Philippians 2:4-5
8 Ephesians 6:1-4

When your family, by their words and actions, point you to Jesus clearly and faithfully, it's important to recognise that, and be grateful for it.[9] And when they don't—

Well, we've already talked about the importance of forgiveness.

It's also important to remember (as difficult as this is) that other people's failure to demonstrate the love of Jesus doesn't get you off the hook for your part.

The benchmark isn't your parents' love, or your siblings' love.

It's the love of Jesus.

In every situation, your role isn't to change other people's hearts or their behaviour. It's to keep trusting that the way of Jesus really is the best way to live, even when the people around you aren't fully living it out.

And I think that's a good place to start if you're trying to figure out how to follow Jesus in a situation where the rest of your family isn't on board.

Of course, you're going to want to *tell* them the good news of Jesus—but like I said in the last chapter, the people we love who don't know Jesus yet don't just need to *hear* about God's love for them; they need to *see* it.

So, yes, tell them about Jesus with your words—but also *show* them the good news of Jesus by the way

---

9 You could literally put this bit into practice right now. What's one specific thing you're grateful to someone in your family for? Take a moment to go thank them for it!

you live your life, by the way you love, honour and respect them.

Humility is key here. Your family might not follow Jesus yet, but they still have all kinds of wisdom and life experience that you don't have; so keep respecting them, listening to them, asking them for help. In the same way that, by God's grace, my faith in Jesus ended up being good news for my sister, let your faith in Jesus be good news for your family.

Whatever your situation, just *keep on following Jesus*. Strive, with God's help, to live a life that demonstrates the truth of what you believe, and trust that God is with you every step of the way.[10]

Lives that demonstrate the truth

When I first started working as a school chaplain, an important-looking man in a suit and tie cornered me at the meet-the-new-staff afternoon tea. He looked me dead in the eye and said, "I need to tell you how important your job is".

He introduced himself as David, the head of the school council—my principal's boss—and he went on to tell this story about how, years ago, he'd had two daughters who went through our school. Somewhere along the way, much to his frustration, they both ended up becoming followers of Jesus after hearing about him from their Christian Studies teachers.

---

10   1 Peter 2:12; Matthew 28:19-20

At first, David was infuriated. He'd sent his kids to this school to get an *education*, not so they could become *Christians*.[11]

But over time, something began to shift.

As David started to investigate Jesus for himself—and, I think, even more importantly, in response to the prayers of his daughters and their steady, faithful commitment to demonstrating the love of Jesus to their dad—David ended up becoming a follower of Jesus too.

He told me the story with tears in his eyes. The love of Jesus, through the love of his daughters, had brought him home into the family of God—and his life had never been the same.

---

11 When I called David to ask for his permission to include this story in the book, he told me he'd even gone as far as replacing his girls' regular bedtime stories with books and articles from atheist philosophers, trying to convince them that God didn't exist.

CHAPTER 11

How to Really Love Your Friends

"For we are God's handiwork, created in Christ Jesus to do good works, which God prepared in advance for us to do."
—*Ephesians 2:10*

If all of God's wisdom for life boils down to loving God and loving others—and if this love is what's supposed to mark us out as followers of Jesus and show the rest of the world what God's love is like—then obviously, one of the key places all of this is going to land for us is in our friendships.

The truth is, being a mediocre friend is pretty easy.

Being a really *good* friend is a whole lot harder.

And so, as a follower of Jesus, how do you build friendships that are strong enough to endure all the ups and downs of life? What should you do when you run into disagreement and conflict? Or when your friend is going through something that's bigger than you know how to handle? Or when they start making choices that you disagree with, or that you're convinced are going to end up hurting them? What should you do when you feel like you and a friend are drifting apart? Or like your friendship is moving in an unhealthy direction?

Obviously, the world is full of opinions about the best answers to all of these questions, and my aim in this short chapter is not to address every possible problem or situation, one by one.

Instead, what I want to do is reframe this whole friendship conversation around the idea from the Bible verse I quoted at the beginning of this chapter: "For we are God's handiwork, created in Christ Jesus to do good works, which God prepared in advance for us to do."

The God of the universe has created you in his image and brought you home to himself on purpose, and for a purpose. He's planted you in your own specific time and place and situation as the *best* person he has in his kingdom to reach out in love to the people he puts in front of you—and, if they don't know Jesus yet, to welcome them home into his family.

And I say all this not to put any kind of pressure on you— not to say, *God's given you a job to do, and you'd better not mess it up!*—but, actually, to say the exact opposite.

Even in the moments in your friendships when you feel like everything's falling apart and you have absolutely zero idea what you're doing, God already has your situation completely under control. He has prepared all kinds of amazing stuff for you to do in your life, and in your friendships—and as you move through each day of your life with Jesus, you can trust him to guide you along, every step of the way.

It's not all up to you. It's all up to him.

Your role is to partner with the God of all love in what he's already doing to love the world. As I once heard author and pastor Jon Tyson put it, it's about walking into every room with the same question: "God, where have you already been working to grow your kingdom and demonstrate your love—and how can I get on board with that?"

Okay, but how do we actually *do* that?

Well, the general answer is to just keep letting God grow you up, day by day, into more and more of his wisdom, in all the ways we've talked about already. But to get slightly more specific, let me share a few starting points that I think are particularly helpful.

Be present

When it comes to loving your friends, I think step one is just being there—being fully present with the people who are in front of you. Which might sound obvious, but when you stop and think about it, it's an increasingly rare gift.

Way back in 1998, a tech writer and consultant named Linda Stone coined the term *continuous partial attention* to describe the growing trend she'd observed of people constantly dividing their attention between multiple different tasks.[1]

Instead of giving their full attention to whoever they were having lunch with, people were using these new things called mobile phones to answer a call or send a text, right there at the table. Instead of being fully present with the person they were with, they were increasingly using technology to scan for *other* opportunities, *other* options, *other* people to connect with.

This was back in the day when phones had tiny black-and-white screens and physical buttons and could only hold 15 text messages at a time, well before iPhones or social media.

We have come a long way since 1998.

And you might think, "This is just how we communicate now".

And, sure, that's true.

But my question is, what is this new normal *doing* to us?

Obviously, digital communication is not all bad; but just as obviously, it's no substitute for the real thing—a reality we experience every time we try to talk to one of our friends about something that really matters to us, and then look up to find them checking their notifications.

---

1 ETech Keynote by Linda Stone, 7 March 2006, http://radar.oreilly.com/2006/03/etech-linda-stone-1.html (accessed 27 Jan. 2024).

When we look at the life of Jesus, we find him modelling a completely different way of living. No matter how busy Jesus got, no matter how many demands there were on his time, he always gave his full attention to whoever was right in front of him.

If you've experienced this kind of attention, you know what a profound expression of love and care it is. In our digital-technology-saturated world, one of the most powerful, counter-cultural gifts you can give your friends is your full, undivided attention.

If you're looking for a place to start, here's a small but radical suggestion for you: the next time you're hanging out with friends, put your phone on Do Not Disturb and leave it in your bag.[2]

Let the people you're *actually with* be the people you choose to give your full attention.

Really listen

Now that you're fully present (or, at least, working on it), I think the next key step is to keep growing in your ability to really *listen* to your friends.

Again, this seems pretty straightforward. But the more I reflect on it, the more I realise it cuts right to the heart of how I see my friends—and also, how I see myself.

---

2 At this point, you may be thinking, "But what if there's an emergency?" I'll let you decide for yourself what qualifies as an "emergency", but if your phone is anything like mine, it should allow you to adjust your Do Not Disturb settings so that calls from particular numbers can still get through.

The writer Brennan Manning has helped me to see that when you walk into any social situation, there are basically two ways you can carry yourself:

You can walk into the room, grasping for care and attention, like, "Here I am!"

Or you can walk into the room, ready to *give* care and attention, like, "There you are!"[3]

Now, of course, true friendship involves both giving *and* receiving care and attention—and the way you express either of these attitudes will vary based on your personality. But, like I said, I think it's deeper than this.

Again, go back to the biographies of Jesus in the Bible. Look at how *constantly* compassionate and humble and caring and others-focused he was. Look at how he just *kept on loving* the people around him, no matter what.

How could he do that so consistently?

Simple: he knew who he was.

Jesus knew the deep, relentless love of his Father, not just as an idea but as the heartbeat of his whole life. No matter how busy he got, he always made time to get away by himself, to pray, to focus and refocus on God, to fill up on the abundance of his Father's love. And as a result, he always had plenty to pour out into the lives of the people around him.

---

3 Brennan Manning, *Abba's Child: The Cry of the Heart for Intimate Belonging* (NavPress, 2015), p. 17.

So, what does it look like to be less "here I am" and more "there you are" in our friendships?

Well, like I said, I think listening is key—and the first step here is to let the other person do most of the talking.[4]

Often when we're in a conversation, we might be listening to the other person, but we're spending less time trying to *understand* them and more time trying to figure out what we're going to say next.[5]

When we step back and allow the conversation to be a bit less about us and a bit more about them, that creates space for us to really hear and understand our friends.

This is a deeply loving act, all by itself—but it also helps us to more clearly see all kinds of other ways we might love and care for our friends.

Dealing with conflict

Of course, this stuff is not always smooth sailing, and so the next thing I want to do is share a few thoughts on what to do when you find yourself in situations of conflict.

Let's start with a great piece of general wisdom from the Bible: "Do not let the sun go down while you are still angry."[6]

---

4 To any of my close friends or family who may be reading this book: yes, I am well aware that this is a growth area for me.

5 As the writer Stephen Covey puts it in his book, *The 7 Habits of Highly Effective People* (Free Press, 2004), p. 239: "Most people do not listen with the intent to understand; they listen with the intent to reply. They're either speaking or preparing to speak."

6 Ephesians 4:26

Obviously, there'll be times when you or your friend need time and space to process what's happened before you feel ready to talk about it—and the better you get to know your friends, the more you'll get a sense of when to talk it out and when to back off for a bit. But the general principle here is, *Resolve conflict as soon as you can.*

Don't give things time to spiral out of control. Don't go off and tell your other friends about it so they can join you in your anger. Instead, tell *God* about it. Ask for *his* help to see the situation clearly and resolve it well. And then, as soon as possible, find a time to talk directly to the person you're in conflict with—just between the two of you.[7]

Start by genuinely owning and apologising for your part in the conflict. (My mum once gave me the wise advice that even if you're only responsible for 10% of the situation, you're still 100% responsible for your 10%.)

Then take everything we've seen so far about listening, and about forgiveness, and talk things out as best you can.

You can't control how the other person will respond— and there will still be times when you really *can't* resolve things on your own and you need to bring in some outside help.

But, whatever happens, if you head into the situation trusting in God's love, depending on his help, and dedicated to putting the other person first, you'll be

---

7   Matthew 18:15

giving yourself the best possible chance of coming to a healthy resolution.

A friend your friends can trust

In the end, so much of friendship comes down to trust.

The whole point of this book is to show you why I'm convinced that God can be trusted completely in every area of your life—and so, of course, learning to reflect God's character will mean learning to become trustworthy people ourselves.

This means doing the best we can to keep our word and our commitments.

It means not saying anything when your friend's not in the room that you'd be embarrassed about if they suddenly walked in.

It means being honest and transparent, even when it's uncomfortable.

Which, admittedly, is not how most people live their lives. But it's how Jesus lived his—and the more you let his wisdom guide your friendships, the more you'll become the best possible friend to your friends.

When you're in over your head

This all becomes particularly important when your friends come to you with their problems—especially the problems that are beyond your ability to solve, or to even know *how* to solve.

You may not be able to fix everything. But you can be fully present with your friends. You can listen and empathise with them. You can offer the wisest advice you know how to give.

And when you realise you're both in over your heads, you can reach out for help, because sometimes loving your friends means getting them the support they need from somewhere else—from a parent, a teacher, a doctor, a counsellor, a youth leader, or some other wise adult.

And whatever else you do, keep reaching out for help from the God who made your friends, and who loves them even more than you do—and remember that you can trust him with every situation.

Pray for your friends. Keep praying and don't give up.[8] Bring all your anxiety to Jesus, and know that he cares for both you and your friends.[9]

And pray *with* your friends, even the ones who don't know Jesus yet. You'd be surprised by how many people are grateful to hear you pray for them, even if they're not fully convinced there's anyone out there to pray to.

Our great God is on a mission to redeem and restore and renew the whole universe. All he's asking you to do is to trust him—and then to get out there and love the person in front of you as best you can, knowing that God is willing and able to take care of the rest.

---

8   Luke 18:1; 1 Thessalonians 5:17
9   1 Peter 5:7

CHAPTER 12

Sharing the Good News

"God our Saviour ... wants all people to be saved and to come to the knowledge of the truth."
—1 Timothy 2:3-4

Now we come to one of the most uncomfortable things about following Jesus in our post-Christian culture.

On one hand, if the good news of Jesus really is the best news the world has ever known, then it's way too good to keep to ourselves. If Jesus really has come to welcome us home into abundant life with God, then the most loving thing in the whole world that we can do for our friends is to introduce them to him.

On the other hand, for most of us, for a bunch of the

reasons we've already talked about, sharing our faith with the people around us feels deeply unnatural and uncomfortable.

Trusting Jesus for ourselves is one thing. We might even feel okay about expressing that faith as our own personal, subjective opinion. But when it comes to actually trying to change someone's mind about Jesus, most of us tend to hesitate.

We have this sense that sharing the gospel—telling people the good news of Jesus in a way that suggests it should matter to *them* too—is somehow crossing a line.

But if that's true, it's a line *everyone* is crossing.

Because sharing a gospel is not just something that followers of Jesus do; it's what the whole world does.

I mean, obviously, not everyone is preaching the gospel of *Jesus*—but everyone is preaching a gospel ("good news") about *something*.

Everyone has *some* set of values that they believe are good news for the world, and that they want other people to get on board with.

Some people are preaching the "good news" of atheism. Some are preaching the "good news" of anti-racism, or patriotism, or LGBTQIA pride. Others are preaching the "good news" of vegetarianism or veganism—or the carnivore diet.

There's the gospel of socialism and the gospel of capitalism, the gospel of this or that political party or candidate, the gospel of renewable energy, the gospel of scientific advancement, the gospel of academic achievement, and the age-old gospels of sex, fame, money and power.

There are important conversations to be had about all these issues, and my point right now is not to make a moral judgment about any of them.

It's just to say that, for all of us, the question isn't, *Are you preaching a gospel?*

It's, *Which gospel are you preaching?*[1]

We're all looking for the good life, and we've all got views about what it looks like and how society should get there. And so, consciously or not, *everyone* has some kind of gospel that they're believing and sharing.

Followers of Jesus are just the ones who have come to the conclusion that *he's* the truest, best answer to the same questions that *everyone* is trying to answer.

Resisting religion

I think a big part of why talking about Jesus feels so uncomfortable is that, when most people hear the invitation to follow him, they think we're inviting them to put their trust in a *religion*, rather than what we're really doing, which is inviting them to put their trust in a *person*.

In our post-Christian culture, many people see "organised religion" in general, and Christianity in

---

1 John Mark Comer, *Practicing the Way: Be with Jesus. Become like him. Do as he did* (Waterbrook Press, 2024), p. 153-154.

particular, as weird and outdated and problematic.

I think that's partly thanks to the historical factors we explored back in chapter 5—and also partly just because our culture trains us to be so highly individualistic. We don't like the idea of religious authority figures telling us what to do; we want to set our own destiny.

We also live in an era where we've witnessed the public failures of so many institutions and authority figures— where we've seen all kinds of awful stuff come to light across so many spheres of culture, including the church. And so now, when we invite people to follow Jesus, it can sound like we're inviting people to be a part of all *that*. Which is not what we're doing, obviously, but you can understand why people are resistant.

The good news is that while many people are sceptical of the church, that doesn't mean they're sceptical of their friend who goes to church.[2]

Your friends who don't know Jesus might think Christianity is weird and outdated and problematic— but, since they've kept on being your friends, they apparently still think you're okay.

Which means the clearest, most positive picture many people are going to get of Jesus is *you*.

Gentleness and respect

Here's a starting point from Jesus' disciple, Peter:

---

2 Sam Chan, *How to Talk about Jesus (Without Being That Guy): Personal Evangelism in a Sceptical World* (Zondervan, 2020), p. xiii.

In your hearts revere Christ as Lord. Always be prepared to give an answer to everyone who asks you to give the reason for the hope that you have. But do this with gentleness and respect, keeping a clear conscience, so that those who speak maliciously against your good behaviour in Christ may be ashamed of their slander.[3]

So, step one, move through your everyday life, trusting and following Jesus, letting him fill you with the hope that comes from knowing your true identity as God's deeply loved child.

Then, step two, whenever someone asks you the *reason* for the hope that you have, just gently, respectfully tell them about who Jesus is, and the difference he's made in your life.

You don't need to have all the answers. In fact, there's real power in admitting you *don't* know—because when you do that, you're demonstrating what it looks like to follow Jesus *without* having all the answers. You're showing them that following Jesus isn't about getting a bunch of clever arguments lined up in your brain; it's about putting your trust in a person.

So just call out to Jesus for his help, and then respond to the questions that come your way as clearly and honestly as you know how.

Notice, by the way, that Peter isn't telling anyone to go charging around, shouting the Jesus message at

---

3   1 Peter 3:15-16

people who don't want to hear it; he says to tell the people who *ask*.

He seems to trust that, as Jesus' people keep devoting themselves to loving God and loving their neighbours, people are going to notice. As they see the miracle of Jesus' love lived out in front of them, they're going to start asking the kinds of questions that lead them straight to Jesus.[4]

Merge your universes

This brings us right back to what we saw in chapter 9 about how the best way to show the love of Jesus to the world is *together*—which, the cultural analyst Sam Chan says, is a key piece of the puzzle that our friends are often missing:

> *"One of the major reasons our friends aren't Christians is that they don't belong to a community of friends who also believe in Jesus. It's not primarily because they haven't heard the gospel (they probably haven't, but they already think they know what you believe). It's not because there's not enough evidence for the Christian faith (because no matter how much evidence you produce, they'll explain it away). In many cases, the number one reason our friends aren't Christians is that they don't have any other Christian friends."*[5]

---

4 Lesslie Newbigin put it like this: "Where the Church is faithful to its Lord ... people begin to ask the question to which the gospel is the answer." *The Gospel in a Pluralist Society* (SPCK, 2014), p. 119.

5 Chan, *How to Talk about Jesus (Without Being That Guy)*, p. 8.

In response to this observation, he talks about the idea of *merging our universes*—creating spaces for our friends who follow Jesus to hang out with our friends who don't know Jesus yet.

I see this all the time at my church's youth group. We've worked really hard to make it a fun, safe, welcoming, and inclusive space for *any* young person, whoever they are and whatever they think about Jesus—a place where people feel comfortable to invite their friends.

As people who don't yet follow Jesus come along with their friends, they catch a glimpse of what it looks like to follow Jesus in community, and more often than not, they seem to like what they see.

As they keep showing up, they make new friends. Suddenly, they don't just have *one* friend who follows Jesus; they have ten—and as a result, Jesus becomes more and more real and compelling to them.

And so what might it look like for you to start merging your universes? Are you part of a youth group, a Sunday church gathering, or maybe a lunchtime group at school that feels like a good fit for your friends? If so, why not invite them along next week?

And if you really can't imagine your friends feeling at home in those spaces right now, remember: this stuff doesn't need to happen in a formal church setting. Just figure out something that your church friends and your school friends (or whoever) would enjoy doing together, and do it together.

And whatever you do, don't put too much pressure on it. Don't worry about it; pray about it.[6] You're not trying to trick anyone here, or brainwash them, or sell them anything. All you need to do is create space to show your friends what life is like when you follow Jesus—and trust God with the rest.

Getting on board with what God is doing

Which brings me to the last thing I want to say about all of this, which is to remind you that, as you look for opportunities to share the good news of Jesus with your friends, you're getting on board with what God is *already doing*.

There's this fascinating moment in the book of Acts in the Bible, where two early followers of Jesus named Paul and Barnabas come to a town called Lystra and meet a group of people who have absolutely zero knowledge of the God of the Bible. Take a look at the introduction Paul and Barnabas give them:

> *We are bringing you good news, telling you to turn ...*
> *to the living God, who made the heavens and the earth*
> *and the sea and everything in them. In the past, he*
> *let all nations go their own way. Yet he has not left*
> *himself without testimony: he has shown kindness by*
> *giving you rain from heaven and crops in their seasons;*
> *he provides you with plenty of food and fills your*
> *hearts with joy.*[7]

---

6 Philippians 4:6-7
7 Acts 14:15-17

Notice that, as they call their new friends to turn from their old lives to embrace the good news of Jesus, their starting point is the lives their friends are *already living*—their own felt experience. And then they connect that experience back to God's abundant love and provision.

You know that incredible feeling you get when you take the first bite of a delicious meal? That's the God of the universe declaring his love for you!

Paul and Barnabas seem to trust that God is *already* revealing himself to these people; all they're doing is helping their new friends to join the dots.

Around 1,600 years ago, a North African bishop called Augustine famously put it like this: "You have made us for yourself, O Lord, and our heart is restless until it rests in you."

Our friends—like us, and like everyone else in the world—have needs and longings that can only be fully met in Jesus. We are made for life with God and, one way or another, *everyone* is restless until they find their rest in him.

Ultimately, it's not our job to save anyone. It's all God. But as we pray, and as we live out the way of Jesus both individually and in community, and as we take the opportunities God gives us to share what we believe and how he's been working in our lives, we can trust that he will be at work in us and through us, bringing lost people home to himself.

The power of a praying life

I recently read about a follower of Jesus named D.L. Moody, who lived back in the 19th century, and who spent a huge part of his life telling other people the good news of Jesus.

He also spent a huge part of his life *praying*.

Moody kept this list of 100 friends who didn't know Jesus yet—and every day, he'd pull out his prayer list, and he'd pray for all these friends, that they'd come to know Jesus as their Rescuer and King.

And then every time one of these 100 friends put their trust in Jesus, he'd cross their name off the list—until, at the end of his life, someone found Moody's list and discovered that 96 out of 100 names had been crossed off. Out of the 100 people that D.L. Moody had been praying for, 96 had become followers of Jesus by the time Moody died.

Which is *amazing*, right?

A 96% success rate. You've got to be pretty happy with that.

But it gets even better—because, apparently, the last four people on Moody's list all came along to his funeral. And as they heard about his life, and as they heard about the God he believed in, they were so convicted that they turned to put their trust in Jesus, too.

Which means that by the time Moody's body was lowered into the ground, every single person on his list of 100 people had put their trust in Jesus.

Now, what am I saying here? Am I offering you some kind of personal guarantee that every single person that you pray for will end up putting their trust in Jesus?

No. I'm not God. I don't get to make those kinds of promises. And, ultimately, your friends' relationship with God is between them and God. No one else can make those decisions for them.

What I'm saying is that D.L. Moody trusted God enough to faithfully pray that 100 of his friends would come to know Jesus—and then 100 of his friends came to know Jesus.

And so my question is just this:

What might that same loving, gracious God, who faithfully answered Moody's prayers—the God who knows how to give good gifts to all his children,[8] the God who doesn't want anyone to end up separate from him, but for everyone to turn around and follow Jesus...[9] What might that same loving, gracious God be ready and waiting to do in your life, and in the lives of your friends, through your steady, faithful prayers?

---

8 Matthew 7:7-11
9 Ezekiel 18:23; 1 Timothy 2:4; 2 Peter 3:9

CHAPTER 13

Dealing with Disagreement and Criticism

*"We do not hate the world, we are not protesting it,
we are participating in it with a vision
of the way of Jesus."*
—Jon Tyson & Heather Grizzle

Here's what I find strangely encouraging whenever I face disagreement or criticism as a follower of Jesus: if there were a way to perfectly love our neighbours and share the truth of the gospel *without* running into negativity, I'm pretty sure Jesus would have figured it out.

Throughout his time on earth, Jesus showed perfect love to whoever came across his path. He was so deeply immersed in his Father's love and the wisdom of the

Scriptures that, in every single conversation, he knew exactly what to say and how to say it.

And yet, he still experienced conflict and disagreement.

He was still misunderstood and criticised.

He threw the invitation wide open, but not everyone accepted it.

And so it shouldn't surprise us, as we stumblingly, falteringly follow Jesus, that we experience some of these responses in our own lives.

Still, that doesn't make it any more fun to deal with.

We're right back to that same tension we talked about earlier: believing that the good news of Jesus really is the best news the world has ever known, and yet feeling misunderstood as intolerant or narrow-minded or even hateful; wanting to influence the world around us for the better but unsure how to do it.

So how *do* we do it?

How we live matters

The first thing, as we've explored already, is to just keep on striving to *live* as if the good news of Jesus is true—both individually, and in community alongside other followers of Jesus.

After all, if our words are just words, why should anybody believe them?

The author Brennan Manning once said:

*"The greatest single cause of atheism in the world
today is Christians who acknowledge Jesus with their
lips and walk out the door and deny him by their
lifestyle. That is what an unbelieving world simply
finds unbelievable."* [1]

And I think Jesus' disciple Peter was on a similar page
when he encouraged the early Christians to "live such
good lives" among their neighbours who didn't know
Jesus yet that "though they accuse you of doing wrong,
they may see your good deeds and glorify God on the
day he visits us".[2]

The Bible draws a straight line from the way we live our
lives to our ability to effectively share the good news of
Jesus.

Which makes perfect sense, right? Why would anyone
believe what we say about Jesus if we don't live like we
believe it?

In another New Testament letter, Paul encourages
churches to pray "that we may live peaceful and quiet
lives in all godliness and holiness. This is good, and
pleases God our Saviour, who wants all people to be
saved and to come to a knowledge of the truth."[3]

God isn't asking you to go charging around with a
bullhorn, convincing the world how right you are,
but just to get on with living the kind of peaceful,

---

1   Quoted by Ben Simpson in "The Ragamuffin Legacy", RELEVANT
    Magazine, April 2013, https://relevantmagazine.com/faith/
    ragamuffin-legacy/ (accessed January 30, 2024).

2   1 Peter 2:12

3   1 Timothy 2:2–4

unassuming life that demonstrates the love of Jesus to the people around you.

How we speak matters

Whatever else it means to live like the good news of Jesus is true, it has to mean remembering Jesus' instruction to treat other people the way we'd like to be treated[4]—and nowhere is this more true than when we face criticism and disagreement.

Like we saw before, *everyone* is sharing some kind of gospel. As followers of Jesus, we need to share *his* good news with the same gentleness and respect we'd hope our friends would use when trying to convince us about whatever *they* think is good news.[5]

This means taking time to listen and understand before we speak.

It means not always needing to have the last word but, wherever possible, trying to have *this* conversation in a way that leaves the door open for the *next* conversation.

It means remembering that if we're debating just to win the argument—if we're debating out of *any* motive other than love for God expressed through love for the other person—then we've already lost.

What matters is not just *that* we tell the truth but also *how* we tell the truth. If we're not communicating what we believe with gentleness and respect, in a way that

---

4   Matthew 7:12; Luke 6:31

5   Elmer John Thiessen, *The Scandal of Evangelism: A Biblical Study of the Ethics of Evangelism* (Cascade, 2018), p. 115.

seeks to understand and honour the individual person we're talking to, we're missing the point.[6]

If people are going to misunderstand and criticise us, let it be because we're faithfully representing Jesus, not because we're being unkind or obnoxious; let it be *in spite* of our relentless love, not because that love is missing from either our words or our actions.

Assume it's personal

Speaking of honouring the individual, the next thing I think is incredibly helpful as you run into tricky conversations about faith and life is to *always assume it's personal.*

In my experience, when people ask you or confront you about an issue, they're rarely just asking out of theoretical curiosity; almost always, it's far more personal than that.

They ask how a loving God could allow so much suffering in the world, but their real question is why God let their sister get cancer.

They ask if God hates gay people, but their real question is if you think God loves and accepts their dads.

They ask what the Bible says about trans identities, but their real question is if their friend from school is going to feel safe and welcome at your church.

They ask if you really think Jesus is the only way to God,

---

6   1 Peter 3:15

but their real question is if God will save their Buddhist parents or their atheist best friend.

And those deeper, more personal questions demand a deeper, more personal response. So don't just charge in with a one-size-fits-all answer. Take some time to ask the other person what *they* think about the question they're asking, and why the answer matters to them. Stop and listen long enough to get to the heart of what they're really asking.

You see this all the time in Jesus' life: he didn't give one-size-fits-all help; it was always tailored to the person in front of him.

For example, take Jesus' friends Martha and Mary, and their brother, Lazarus. When Lazarus died, his two sisters came to Jesus with the exact same words—"Lord, if you had been here, my brother would not have died"[7]—and yet Jesus met each of them with a very different response.

What Martha needed most in that moment was a *head* answer—*Jesus, how are you going to solve this problem?*—and so that's what Jesus gave her:

> *Your brother will rise again ... I am the resurrection and the life. The one who believes in me will live, even though they die.*[8]

But Mary was a different person with different needs—and so, for her, Jesus didn't just come in swinging with

---

7   John 11:21, 32
8   John 11:23, 25

a solution. Instead, he stood beside Mary in her grief, weeping with her outside her brother's tomb.[9]

And then, in front of both of them, he brought Lazarus back to life again.[10] In the end, both Martha and Mary saw and trusted that Jesus was who he said he was— but their path *into* that understanding and trust was as different as they were.

Jesus *always* saw past the outward appearance and the surface-level questions, right to the heart of whatever was going on. And loving our friends well means trusting Jesus to help us grow in this same kind of wisdom and discernment.

It means getting to know our friends well enough to share not just "the truth" in general but to say what will be both true and most helpful for *them* to hear, in any given moment.

Keep pointing back to Jesus

And whatever else you do, just *keep pointing people back to Jesus.*

When someone asks me, "How can you say that putting your trust in Jesus is the only way to be saved? That's so narrow and intolerant!" they're asking me a question about *me*, and about what *I* think is true.

And, sure, I can offer my opinion.

I can even offer some pretty good logical arguments.

9   John 11:33-35
10   John 11:43-44

But, in the end, who cares what *I* think is true?

If it's just my opinion versus another person's opinion, then why should the other person change their mind?

Besides, I don't even *want* my friend to change their mind about Jesus based on what *I* believe—or even based on what *Christians* believe.

I want them to change their mind about Jesus because of *Jesus*.

And so rather than telling my friend what *I* think, or what *Christians* say, I'll try to frame my answers more like this: "Look, in the end, it doesn't really matter what I think. But what Jesus said about himself is, 'I am the way and the truth and the life. No one comes to the Father except through me.'[11] He said that all of history was pointing towards his great mission to renew the world and bring God's people back to himself. Which, obviously, are some pretty bold claims. But I've weighed up all the evidence, and I've decided Jesus is worth trusting—which means I trust him about this too."

What I'm trying to do here is move from a posture of facing off against each other, pitting what I believe against what they believe, to a posture of standing side by side with the other person, looking together at what Jesus taught.

Because as Sam Chan points out, if we get dragged into an "us versus them" argument, all we're going to do is push each other further away. He says sharing your

---

11 John 14:6

faith should be less about pointing out how right we are and how wrong they are, and more about pointing out what we *all* have in common: that we're all broken human beings, trying to figure this stuff out—and that we all need Jesus to rescue us.[12]

Of course, if you want to be able to tell people what Jesus said, it's pretty helpful to actually *know* what Jesus said—which brings us back to the importance of putting aside regular time to immerse yourself in the Bible.

One of the most helpful things I've started doing over the past couple of years, both for my own friendship with Jesus and my ability to tell other people about him, has been to just keep reading his four biographies in the Bible—Matthew, Mark, Luke and John—over and over again, a chapter or two each day. Whatever else I'm reading in the Bible, I'm always reading the Gospels too.

I've discovered that the deeper I go, the more interesting and rewarding it gets—and the more easy I find it to steer conversations away from my own personal takes on things to the wisdom of Jesus.

Nothing left to prove

Here's a reality of life with Jesus that I'm still coming to grips with but that I'm absolutely convinced is true:

It's actually okay if people think we're backwards and wrong.[13]

---

12 Chan, *How to Talk about Jesus (Without Being That Guy)*, p 130-131.
13 Matthew 5:11-12

I mean, it's not *fun*. It's not something to strive for. And if what we're *actually* catching heat for is our own failure to love our neighbours, then that's obviously not something to be proud of.

But as one writer put it, "Christians, of all people, should have no fear of being viewed as wrong. We are not self-justified people; we are Jesus-justified people."[14] Trusting in Jesus means remembering that we have nothing left to prove, and no one left to prove ourselves to.

Jesus hasn't sent his people out into the world to win arguments for him.

He's sent us out into the world to announce the good news of his kingdom, and to demonstrate that good news to everyone we meet, in the same way Jesus did: by gently, respectfully, persistently loving the person in front of us.

As long as we keep doing that, we can rest assured that we're on the right track.

---

14 Stephen McAlpine, *Being the Bad Guys: How to Live for Jesus in a World That Says You Shouldn't* (The Good Book Company, 2022), p. 74.

CHAPTER 14

Putting It All Together

"But Mary treasured up all these things and pondered them in her heart."
—Luke 2:19

We've covered a lot of ground in this book—but ultimately, like I said right back at the beginning, every question we've been asking has been aimed at helping us answer the one all-important question:

Can I trust him?

In all of the complexity of life, can you really count on Jesus to lead you and guide you and pull you through?

I'm hopeful that some of what you've read might have helped convince you that you can. And so, to finish, I want to look at an example from Luke's biography of

Jesus that I think will help draw things together for us.

Let's zoom in on Mary, the mother of Jesus—because I think her response to the good news of Jesus gives us a great insight into what the faith we've been talking about all through this book can look like.

Faith looks like leaning in

By the time we meet Mary in Luke's Gospel, God's plans are already in motion. Mary's relative Elizabeth is six months pregnant with John the Baptist, the child who will grow up to announce Jesus' arrival to the world—and now God has deployed his messenger, the angel Gabriel, to make another surprise announcement to another unsuspecting mother.[1]

Meanwhile, Mary has her own plans in motion. She's engaged to Joseph, planning her life together with him,[2] with no idea in the world that God's agenda is about to come crashing into hers.

Suddenly, Gabriel appears: "Greetings, you who are highly favoured! The Lord is with you."[3]

And Luke tells us that "Mary was greatly troubled at his words and wondered what kind of greeting this might be".[4]

This response from Mary gives us our first glimpse at what biblical faith looks like: for followers of Jesus,

---

1 Luke 1:26
2 Luke 1:27
3 Luke 1:28
4 Luke 1:29

faith looks like leaning in with your whole heart and your whole mind.

Being "greatly troubled" is a *heart* response. Mary is bringing her full emotional self to the situation—and freaking out the same way any of the rest of us would.

But "wondering" is a *head* response. Timothy Keller points out that "wondered" might be a slightly misleading translation here—because the original Greek word means more than just, *Hmm... I wonder.* It means "to make an audit". It's an *accounting* word, about adding things up, weighing and pondering. Mary is being intensely thoughtful and rational here.[5] She's bringing her full *intellectual* self to the situation too.

People often talk about *faith* and *evidence* as if they're opposite ends of a see-saw—the more evidence you have, the less faith you need; the more faith you have, the less you care about the evidence—but this couldn't be further from a biblical understanding.

The Greek word that gets translated "faith" in our English Bibles doesn't mean believing *in spite* of logical arguments and evidence; it means being persuaded *by* logical arguments and evidence. It means following the evidence, seeing where it leads, and putting your trust in *that*.

Which is exactly what we find Mary doing here. She's present, thoughtful—and deeply troubled by the sudden appearance of an angel in her room!

---

5 Timothy Keller, *Hidden Christmas: The Surprising Truth behind the Birth of Christ* (Hodder and Stoughton, 2018), p. 81.

But Gabriel tells her she has nothing to fear: "Do not be afraid, Mary; you have found favour with God."[6]

This collision of her plans and God's plans isn't a sign of God's anger but of his *favour*.

Which, just as a side note, might be something you need to hear today too. If you're putting your trust in Jesus, you can rest assured that you have found favour with God—that God the Father loves you with the same love he has for Jesus himself.

So don't be afraid. Whatever pain or disruption you're going through, it isn't a sign of God's anger, or his absence. It might even be what it was for Mary: an invitation to put your own agenda aside in order to take the next step into God's less comfortable, far better plan.

Faith looks like asking questions

Gabriel goes on to make some huge promises to Mary.

Miraculously, Mary is going to have a baby. He's going to be called Jesus—meaning "God saves"—and he'll be the answer to all God's promises through all of history to bless and rescue his people.[7]

For Mary, choosing to lean into God's plans for her life is going to be costly and disruptive and *absolutely worth it*, because God has chosen her for a pivotal role in the redemption of the world.

---

6   Luke 1:30
7   Luke 1:31-33

But, naturally, Mary has some questions. For example: "How will this be ... since I am a virgin?"[8]

This may have all happened 2,000 years ago, but people still understood where babies came from.

Which brings us to the next thing Mary teaches us about trust:

For followers of Jesus, faith means asking the big questions with an open mind.

Some people have been handed this toxic version of faith that says, "If you really believed, you wouldn't need to ask so many questions". But clearly, this wasn't Mary's attitude.

But also notice *how* Mary approached her questions.

She didn't sit back with her arms crossed and say, *I'm not believing a word of this until you tell me everything I want to know.*

She didn't close her mind—she *opened* it, asking a thoughtful, information-gathering question: *This should be impossible—so how will it happen?*[9]

In response, Gabriel tells her that God's promises will be fulfilled the way they always have been: not through human strength but through God's grace and power.

Gabriel invites Mary to consider the evidence. God has already started doing the impossible here: "Even Elizabeth your relative is going to have a child in her old

---

8 Luke 1:34
9 Luke 1:34

age, and she who was said to be unable to conceive is in her sixth month."[10]

And then the angel sums it all up with these words: "For no word from God will ever fail."[11]

It's an invitation to Mary to consider not just the evidence in *this* situation, but to look back through history and recognise the truth: that God has never failed—and he's not going to start with her.

Faith looks like trusting in God's character

Which brings us to the last thing I want to point out here: for followers of Jesus, faith looks like trusting in God's character.

Think about it: why do you put your trust in *anyone*?

Because of their character, and their track record.

Because their *past* actions convince you that they're the kind of person who can be trusted in the *present* and the *future*.

Gabriel reminds Mary that God's track record is absolutely spotless, perfect and unbroken. He's proven time and time again that he's well worth trusting.

And so Mary trusts him.

"I am the Lord's servant," she says. "May your word to me be fulfilled."[12]

---

10 Luke 1:36
11 Luke 1:37
12 Luke 1:38

What she *doesn't* say is, *Perfect! All my questions have suddenly been answered! This whole situation is totally cool and normal now!*

Things were still bizarre and uncertain and hard to process.

But Mary leant in with her full heart and mind.

She asked questions. She weighed the evidence.

She considered God's character and track record.

She put all that together, and came to the most rational, reasonable conclusion: *I can trust God with this.*

And moving forward, after Jesus' birth and all the strange things that happened around that, Luke tells us that "Mary treasured up all these things and pondered them in her heart".[13]

She didn't just stay where she was. She kept on learning and growing and figuring things out.

She was still on the journey of learning to trust. But she was on the journey *with God*—and that made all the difference.

"Do you think you can trust him?"

Way back at the beginning of this book, I talked about that teenager from my youth group who came to see me, weighed down with questions, and with the overwhelming complexity of life.

---

13 Luke 2:19

We talked for a while about some of those specific questions, and I did my best to provide some helpful, concrete answers—because I really do think all those conversations are so important.

But eventually, I stopped and pointed out what was already becoming obvious to both of us: we were never going to get to the bottom of all the questions; they were endless—not because God is elusive, but because he's *infinite*.

"Listen," I said, "all these questions are so important and worthwhile, and I'm so happy to keep talking about them—but in the end, I think there's only one thing you really *need* to figure out: Do you think Jesus loves you? Do you think you can trust him?"

He thought about it for a while, and then his eyes narrowed, and he nodded.

"Yeah," he said slowly. "I think he does. And I think I can."

And I saw the weight begin to lift from his shoulders.

Not because all the other questions had magically fallen away, or become unimportant, but because his focus had shifted from arguments and ideas back to Jesus himself.

Jesus who, throughout his entire life, had never failed to completely, perfectly love the person in front of him.

Jesus who, at the cross, had already shown just how far he's willing to go to welcome his lost children home to himself.

Jesus who, through his resurrection, had proven that not even death can stop him—that love, hope, joy and abundant life really are where the whole universe is headed.

Jesus who, for every time this friend of mine might mess up or fall short or continue to get it wrong, would be right there waiting with wide-open arms and grace upon grace upon grace.

Jesus who, for all the questions and doubts that might still be unanswered for now, had already shown that he really could be trusted.

A final word

My great hope and prayer for you, as you finish this book, is that you'll let Jesus take that same weight off *your* shoulders.

May you lean all the way into faith in Jesus, bringing all your fear and doubt and pain and confusion with you—and may you discover for yourself that his love is vast enough to handle *all* of it.

May you plant yourself like a tree by the steady stream of his love and grace and wisdom.

May you learn, day by day, to embrace the reality that what he wants for you is only, ever, always, your deepest, truest happiness.

And may you know, right down to the depths of your soul, that you really can trust him.

Can I Really Believe in This Stuff?

*"There is a resurrection-shaped dent in the
historical record, and it's quite a puzzle
working out how it got there."*
—John Dickson

Throughout this book, I've been trying to help grow your confidence that following Jesus really is worth it—that Jesus shows us a God we can trust, even in the middle of the most complex, confusing, and difficult situations life can throw at us.

But of course, all of that falls apart if it turns out that the Jesus message isn't actually *true*. And so, even though a full explanation of the historical evidence for the life, death, and resurrection of Jesus is beyond the scope of this book, I wanted to at least give you a brief overview, here at the end.

The all-important question

As far as I can see, the whole Christian faith stands or falls on one question:

Did Jesus really rise from the dead?

Because, sure, Jesus *claimed* to be the one true God of the universe,[1] here to offer us eternal life beyond the grave by dying and rising again[2]—but anyone can *say* those things.

If Jesus didn't follow through with the coming-back-to-life part, then he's just another human being who died and stayed dead. As the Bible itself puts it: "If Christ has not been raised, our preaching is useless and so is your faith."[3]

But if Jesus really *did* come back to life in the middle of human history, that proves he really is who he claimed to be—because what else but the power of God could bring a dead person back to life again?

Did Jesus actually exist?

But before we tackle the question of Jesus' resurrection, we should probably figure out whether Jesus even existed in the first place.

---

1   John 10:30, 14:9
2   John 11:25-26; 14:6; Luke 18:31-34; 24:46-47
3   1 Corinthians 15:14

You might assume that the Bible is our only source of evidence here, but there are actually several other ancient historical sources that can help us out.

Jesus is mentioned in the *Annals*, a history of the Roman Empire written by the Roman historian, Tacitus, who was born less than 30 years after Jesus died. He shows up in *Jewish Antiquities*, a history of the Jewish people written by the Jewish historian, Josephus, who was born less than *ten* years after Jesus died. He also gets a mention in an ancient letter written by the Roman governor Pliny the Younger, and in a handful of other ancient writings.

Put all that together and here's what history tells us about Jesus before we even open a Bible:

- He is a legitimate historical figure who actually existed.

- He had a brother named James.

- He lived in Israel while Tiberius Caesar was emperor of Rome and Pontius Pilate was governor of Judea.

- He had a reputation for being a wise teacher and a performer of miracles.[4]

- His followers called him "the Christ", claiming he was a king.

---

4 Whether Jesus *actually* performed miracles is outside the scope of ancient history—but historians are confident that the ancient eyewitnesses to Jesus' life saw him do things that *they* believed were miracles.

- He was arrested in Jerusalem at around the time of the Jewish Passover festival, and executed on a cross, on Pontius Pilate's orders.

- After his death, reports spread that he'd come back to life and showed himself to his followers.

- As a result, people not only kept following Jesus, they worshipped him—and instead of shrinking and disappearing, the number of Jesus' followers increased exponentially.

In 2014, historian and author John Dickson put out a public challenge: "I will eat a page of my Bible if someone can find me just one full Professor of Ancient History, Classics, or New Testament in an accredited university somewhere in the world ... who thinks Jesus never lived."[5]

All these years later, his Bible is still intact. Whatever doubts they might have about particular details of his life, historians are united on at least this much: Jesus isn't just a myth; he really did exist.

New Testament sources

As helpful as Josephus and Tacitus might be in establishing Jesus' existence, by far our best and most detailed information about Jesus comes from the collection of 27 ancient texts we find gathered together in the New Testament of our Bibles.

---

5 John Dickson, "I'll eat a page from my Bible if Jesus didn't exist", https://www.abc.net.au/news/2014-10-17/dickson-ill-eat-a-page-from-my-bible-if-jesus-didnt-exist/5820620 (accessed 6 Jan. 2024).

Which, of course, immediately raises an objection: *But those texts are completely biased! They're religious writings! How can we trust them to give us legitimate historical information about Jesus?*

And, sure, the writings of the New Testament are biased—but as any decent historian will tell you, *so is every other text*. Every writer has their own agenda or point of view. The solution isn't to throw out every biased text (because then you'd have to throw out pretty much everything); it's to *understand* each text's bias and take it into account when you're evaluating the information.

The writers of the Bible *absolutely* want to convince you that Jesus is who he says he is—and that he really did rise from the dead. They couldn't be more open about it.[6] The question is, *Are the claims they're making about Jesus actually true?*

And the good news is, there are plenty of solid reasons to trust that they are.

Credible eyewitness testimony

Let's stick with the main claim, which is also the most outlandish one: that Jesus rose from the dead.

To start weighing the evidence for that claim, first we need to take a moment to consider what *kind* of evidence we're dealing with when we're trying to assess the possibility of a resurrection.

---

6 See, for example, Luke 1:1-4; John 20:30-31; 1 Corinthians 15:1-8; 1 John 1:1-4.

We're not looking for *scientific* evidence; we can't stick Jesus in a lab and run the experiment a few more times. Jesus' resurrection, if it happened, was a one-off historical event—which means that this is more like solving a crime than testing a scientific hypothesis.

Here's John Dickson again:

> *"The evidence for the resurrection boils down to testimony that is early, widespread, and credible. It is not the sort of testimony we would expect if the resurrection were a late-developing legend; nor if it were a fraud. It is, instead, the kind of testimony we would expect if the first Christians really did find an empty tomb and really did experience what they took to be sightings of Jesus alive after his death."*[7]

Let's break that down a bit.

First, the claim that Jesus rose from the dead is *early*. The New Testament texts were written down within living memory of Jesus, while the original eyewitnesses to his life were still alive.

We also have *thousands* of ancient manuscript copies of these documents—far more than we have for any ancient text. Historians can compare these with each other to confirm that the New Testament hasn't been changed or edited over time.

This rules out the idea that the resurrection claim is just a legend that developed over the decades and centuries

---

7 John Dickson, *Is Jesus History?* (The Good Book Company, 2019), p. 110.

following Jesus' death. Right from the beginning, Jesus' disciples were claiming to have seen him alive again from the dead.

The claim that Jesus rose from the dead is also *widespread*. It doesn't just show up in a single text. We have multiple independent eyewitnesses—multiple eyewitnesses we can be confident didn't just copy each other's information—all making the same claim.

And these multiple independent claims are also *credible*. They're not based on third- or fourth-hand information. The New Testament documents were written down either *by* the original eyewitnesses themselves, or by close associates of those eyewitnesses. There's also no clear reason to believe these accounts are fabricated, and (as we'll see in a bit) plenty of reason to trust that the original eyewitnesses were telling the truth.

The empty tomb

So, with all that said, let me lay out the crime scene for you—the pieces of the puzzle that we need to find a way to explain, one way or another.

On a Thursday evening, sometime around the year AD 30, Jesus was arrested and put on trial, at which point his disciples ran off and deserted him.

Jesus was crucified on Friday by the Roman authorities. Following his death, a wealthy man by the name of Joseph of Arimathea asked for Jesus' body in order to give him a proper burial. He buried Jesus in his own tomb.

The religious authorities who'd demanded Jesus' death in the first place knew that he'd been telling his disciples he was going to rise from the dead. Obviously, they didn't think this was actually going to happen—but following Jesus' burial, they had the tomb sealed shut and posted guards outside to keep anyone from stealing the body and *claiming* he'd come back to life.

But then somehow, by Sunday morning, the tomb was empty.

How do we explain that?

Well, of course, the religious authorities claimed that the disciples had stolen Jesus' body—but weren't they the ones who'd just taken extensive steps to ensure this *couldn't happen*?

And if Jesus' disciples hadn't been willing to stick around to defend his *living* body when he got arrested, why would they risk their lives in a mission to defend his *dead* body?

The disciples had another explanation for the empty tomb: they claimed Jesus had come back to life. They said they'd seen him, touched him, spoken to him, eaten with him—and what's so compelling about *their* story is that every single one of them stuck to it for the rest of their lives, even when they were threatened with violence, imprisonment and death.

The same people who'd had Jesus arrested and killed in the first place wanted nothing more than to stamp out the rumours of his resurrection. Again and again, they brought Jesus' disciples face to face with the same choice: *Deny the resurrection or we'll kill you.*

And again and again, the disciples stuck to their story: *Jesus is the risen King of the universe. Kill us if you have to—it won't be the end of us—but we can't deny what we saw.*

How do we explain that?

Unlikely eyewitnesses

Meanwhile, it wasn't just Jesus' original crew of disciples who claimed they'd seen him alive again.

We also have the testimony of Paul, a religious leader who started out persecuting Jesus' followers for spreading the claim of his resurrection—and then flipped and became a follower of Jesus himself.

Why?

Well, the reason he gave was, *I saw him alive again.*[8]

Then there's the testimony of Jesus' own brothers, who started out assuming (as you would) that their brother was out of his mind for the claims he was making—and then became believers *after* Jesus died.[9]

Why?

Again, the reason they gave was, *We saw him alive again.*[10]

---

8 1 Corinthians 15:8
9 Mark 3:20-21; James 1:1; Jude 1:1
10 1 Corinthians 15:7

There were hundreds of other eyewitnesses who said the same thing.[11]

How do we explain that?

Pick your miracle

Then there's the fact that we're even still talking about *any* of this.

Jesus wasn't the only teacher in 1st-century Israel who gathered a bunch of followers by claiming to be God's chosen one. There were at least a dozen other would-be kings of Israel who did the exact same thing. But then the Romans killed them—and as you'd expect, everyone stopped following them, because who wants to devote their lives to a failed, dead, would-be king?

So the question is, what was so different about Jesus? Why did his followers keep right on following him after he died? Why did the number of Jesus' followers grow exponentially, even when following Jesus came with suffering and persecution? Why, 2,000 years after Jesus was put in the ground, are there still *billions* of people alive today who self-identify as Christians?

How do we explain that?

Obviously, the resurrection is a massive claim. But so is the claim that an obscure homeless dead guy from 2,000 years ago somehow transformed all of human history; that would be its own kind of miracle.

---

11 1 Corinthians 15:6

So which of those two miracles are you going to choose to believe?[12]

Keep digging deeper

Can I *prove* to you that Jesus rose from the dead?

Of course not. I can't prove *any* event from ancient history to the point where you couldn't deny it if you wanted to.

Here's what I think is a more helpful question: Does the resurrection make good sense of the evidence in front of us? Does it make *more* sense than the alternatives?

I think it does.

Ultimately, though, you're going to need to decide for yourself what you make of it all. There's plenty more evidence to uncover, and I'd encourage you to keep digging through it.[13]

As you keep investigating it all with an open mind, I'm confident that, by the grace of our loving God, you'll discover the truth for yourself. You'll find that Jesus is not only *real* but exactly who he says he is: gracious, kind, absolutely life-transforming—and well worth trusting.

---

12 Scrivener, *The Air We Breathe*, p. 218.

13 If you're interested, I've written a little book called *How Do We Know That Christianity Is Really True?* (The Good Book Company, 2021), which goes through all this stuff in more detail. You could also check out John Dickson's excellent book, *Is Jesus History?*, which I've already referenced a couple of times in this chapter.

Discussion Guide

Chapter 1: Life to the full

1. "It's a pretty rough time to be a young person." Do you agree? Why or why not?

2. Which of the issues highlighted in this chapter feel like the biggest ones to you?

3. When do you feel the most confident that following Jesus is worth it? When do you most struggle to believe it?

Chapter 2: The most important discovery

1. Which part of Chris' description of God's love most struck you?

2. Were there any parts where you were thinking, "Yes, but what about...?" What were they, and how come?

3. Can you think of any specific stories from the Gospels where Jesus shows us the love of God lived out in the ways described on page 22? (If you're stuck, try: Mark 10:46-52; Luke 7:36-50; John 13:1-5.)

4. Do you ever think of Jesus as the good, loving guy and God the Father as mean and spiteful (like on page 23)? What did you read in this chapter that counters that idea?

Chapter 3: The good news about God's judgment

1. In what ways do you struggle with the idea of God's judgment? What did you find most helpful in this chapter?

2. This chapter described sin as "unwillingness to trust that what God wants for me is only my deepest happiness". How did that look for the first man and woman? How does that look for you now?

3. Did you identify with Chris' description of "a firehose of beauty and brokenness that comes blasting at us every single day"? Where have you seen beauty and brokenness around you this week?

4. Why is Jesus our only hope for justice?

Chapter 4: Better than you think

1. How do you think you would have summarised the "good news" before you read this chapter? What about now?

2. What are you tempted to see your fundamental identity as? What difference does it make to remember that, fundamentally, you are "made in the image of God"?

3. Look up one of the verses referenced on page 50. What excites you about the way God's story is going to end?

4. If you're one of Jesus' disciples, what could you do to join with him in the renewal of the world? Think about something you could do today; this month; this year. Use the questions on page 52 to help.

Chapter 5: How did we get here?

1. Have you felt the kind of tension that comes from following Jesus that's described at the start of this chapter? When?

2. Did you learn anything new from this chapter? How would you explain it to someone else? What questions do you still have about it?

3. "Most people who don't believe that Christianity is true still kind of live as if it's true. They're still holding on to a bunch of Jesus' ideas and values." Do you agree? Why or why not?

4. Which parts of following Jesus do you think our culture approves of (and sees as "common sense")? Which parts do you think our culture disapproves of (and thinks Christians are on the wrong side of progress)?

Chapter 6: Living like it's true

1. On pages 67-68, Chris says that for us to keep trusting and following Jesus, we're going to need to be confident about three things: that the good news of Jesus is good, true, and actually works in real life. Which of those are you most and least confident in?

2. How would you describe what wisdom is, based on this chapter?

3. What do you find hard about reading the Bible? Which of Chris' five questions on pages 74-76 did you find most helpful?

4. Have you ever come up against stuff in the Bible that you disagree with? What have you read in this chapter that could help you process that?

Chapter 7: Who are you becoming?

1. Talk honestly about your tech use. In what ways is it shaping you, do you think?

2. Are there any habits that you want to start, based on this chapter?

3. Are there any habits that you want to stop or change, to prevent you from being distracted from following Jesus? How can we help one another?

4. In what ways have you already seen God transforming you into the image of Jesus? What would you like him to change next?

Chapter 8: Disappointment and disaster

1. Do you know people like the ones described on pages 96-97—whose experience of suffering and tragedy has either driven them away from God or drawn them closer to him?

2. "Deleting God from the equation isn't going to take your pain away. If anything, it's going to do the opposite." Do you agree? Why or why not?

3. Chris writes that Jesus is "God's truest, best, most complete answer to all our questions about suffering". What does he mean? How does looking at Jesus help us when we suffer?

4. Is there any area of fear, doubt, disappointment or frustration with God that you're processing at the moment? How could we pray about that together?

Chapter 9: How to change the world

1. "Personal faith is mostly still welcome in our post-Christian culture, as long as you keep it to yourself. But ... when you start talking about Jesus' teachings like they're not just opinions but the truth—that's when people get a whole lot less comfortable." Have you experienced that to be the case? If so, what did you find helpful in this chapter?

2. Look at the four options for engaging with culture laid out on pages 109-113. How have you seen those play out among Christians you know? Which one do you think you naturally tend towards, and why?

3. Chris says that the way to change the world is through "the family of Jesus' people, loving one another and welcoming the world to join us". If you're part of a church, what do you appreciate about it? What do you find hard?

4. "What might it look like to take the next step deeper into community with Jesus' people?" Consider Chris' questions on pages 114-115 and make a plan.

Chapter 10: How to live with your family

1. On page 119, Chris writes that when Jesus talks about love, he's mostly talking about an action, rather than a feeling. Do you agree that this makes loving your family seem more achievable? Why or why not?

2. What did you find most helpful in the section about forgiveness?

3. If you have siblings, what could loving action towards them look like this week?

4. Consider the adults in your household. What could loving action and honour towards them look like this week?

Chapter 11: How to really love your friends

1. "The truth is, being a mediocre friend is pretty easy. Being a really good friend is a whole lot harder." When have you found that to be true? What are the key differences between a mediocre friend and a good one, do you think?

2. Read Ephesians 2:10. What do you find encouraging about this verse as you think about friendship?

3. This chapter talked about the importance of being present, listening well, dealing with conflict, being trustworthy, and knowing when to reach out for help. Which of those are you currently best at, do you think? Which of those do you struggle with the most? What does that tend to look like?

4. Going forward, what's one thing you want to do differently when it comes to your friendships?

Chapter 12: Sharing the good news

1. "Everyone is preaching a gospel about something." What kind of alternative "gospels" do people you know preach? What makes the gospel of Jesus different?

2. What is it that you'd most like to share with your friends about who Jesus is and the difference he's made in your life? If you had the opportunity to say anything, what would you say?

3. What did you think about the idea of "merging your universes"? What might that look like for you? Then plan to make it happen.

4. Write a list of people you'd like to put their trust in Jesus. (It doesn't have to be as long as D.L. Moody's!) Then pray for them together.

Chapter 13: Dealing with disagreement and criticism

1. Have you ever faced disagreement or criticism as a follower of Jesus? What happened? How did you respond?

2. Which piece of advice in this chapter did you find most helpful and why? What questions do you still have?

3. Think back to the situation you talked about in question 1. Next time, what would it look like to engage in the way outlined in this chapter? What sort of things could you say, do, or ask?

Chapter 14: Putting it all together

1. Mary shows us that faith looks like leaning in and asking questions. What questions has this book helped you with? What questions do you want to keep pondering as you move forward?

2. Mary shows us that faith looks like trusting God's character. What are the things that God has done (in the Bible or in your own life) that give you the most confidence as you look back?

3. "In the end, I think there's only one thing you really need to figure out: Do you think Jesus loves you? Do you think you can trust him?" Where are you in your journey towards figuring out your answer?

4. Thinking back over the whole book, what do you most want to remember about why following Jesus is worth it?